# IOS FORENSICS 101

## EXTRACTING LOGICAL AND PHYSICAL DATA FROM IPHONE, IPAD AND MAC OS

## 4 BOOKS IN 1

**BOOK 1**
IOS FORENSICS 101: INTRODUCTION TO DIGITAL INVESTIGATIONS

**BOOK 2**
IOS FORENSICS 101: TECHNIQUES FOR EXTRACTING LOGICAL DATA

**BOOK 3**
IOS FORENSICS 101: MASTERING PHYSICAL DATA ACQUISITION

**BOOK 4**
IOS FORENSICS 101: EXPERT ANALYSIS AND CASE STUDIES

## ROB BOTWRIGHT

*Published by Rob Botwright*
*Library of Congress Cataloging-in-Publication Data*
*ISBN 978-1-83938-806-4*
*Cover design by Rizzo*

## Disclaimer

*The contents of this book are based on extensive research and the best available historical sources. However, the author and publisher make no claims, promises, or guarantees about the accuracy, completeness, or adequacy of the information contained herein. The information in this book is provided on an "as is" basis, and the author and publisher disclaim any and all liability for any errors, omissions, or inaccuracies in the information or for any actions taken in reliance on such information. The opinions and views expressed in this book are those of the author and do not necessarily reflect the official policy or position of any organization or individual mentioned in this book. Any reference to specific people, places, or events is intended only to provide historical context and is not intended to defame or malign any group, individual, or entity. The information in this book is intended for educational and entertainment purposes only. It is not intended to be a substitute for professional advice or judgment. Readers are encouraged to conduct their own research and to seek professional advice where appropriate. Every effort has been made to obtain necessary permissions and acknowledgments for all images and other copyrighted material used in this book. Any errors or omissions in this regard are unintentional, and the author and publisher will correct them in future editions.*

# BOOK 1 - IOS FORENSICS 101: INTRODUCTION TO DIGITAL INVESTIGATIONS

# BOOK 2 - IOS FORENSICS 101: TECHNIQUES FOR EXTRACTING LOGICAL DATA

# BOOK 3 - IOS FORENSICS 101: MASTERING PHYSICAL DATA ACQUISITION

# BOOK 4 - IOS FORENSICS 101: EXPERT ANALYSIS AND CASE STUDIES

## Introduction

Welcome to "iOS Forensics 101: Extracting Logical and Physical Data from iPhone, iPad, and Mac OS," a comprehensive book bundle designed to immerse you in the intricate world of digital investigations within Apple's ecosystem. Across four essential volumes, this collection serves as your definitive guide to mastering the art and science of iOS forensics, equipping you with the knowledge and tools necessary to navigate the complexities of extracting, analyzing, and presenting digital evidence.

In "iOS Forensics 101: Introduction to Digital Investigations," Book 1 sets the stage by introducing foundational concepts and principles critical to understanding the landscape of digital forensics. From exploring the unique challenges posed by IOS devices to delving into legal considerations and best practices, this volume provides a solid framework for embarking on your journey into iOS forensic analysis.

Book 2, "iOS Forensics 101: Techniques for Extracting Logical Data," dives deeper into practical methodologies and tools used to extract and scrutinize logical data from iPhones, iPads, and Mac OS devices. Whether navigating iCloud backups, analyzing application data, or uncovering user-generated content, this volume equips you with essential techniques to uncover valuable evidence while maintaining forensic rigor.

In Book 3, "iOS Forensics 101: Mastering Physical Data Acquisition," you will explore advanced strategies for acquiring comprehensive physical images of iOS devices. Through detailed exploration of tools such as GrayKey, Cellebrite UFED, and Checkm8, this volume enhances your proficiency in bypassing device security measures, accessing encrypted data, and capturing detailed device images crucial for in-depth forensic analysis.

Finally, Book 4, "iOS Forensics 101: Expert Analysis and Case Studies," brings theory into practice with real-world applications, expert insights, and detailed case studies. By examining diverse scenarios—from cybercrimes to corporate investigations—this volume illustrates how forensic methodologies translate into actionable intelligence and courtroom-ready evidence. Each case study provides invaluable insights into the application of forensic techniques in solving complex digital investigations.

Whether you are new to the field or a seasoned professional, "iOS Forensics 101" empowers you to navigate the evolving landscape of digital investigations with confidence and proficiency. As technology continues to evolve and digital footprints expand, this book bundle remains your indispensable resource for mastering iOS forensic methodologies, contributing to the pursuit of justice, and ensuring integrity in the investigation of digital evidence.

**BOOK 1**
*IOS FORENSICS 101*
*INTRODUCTION TO DIGITAL INVESTIGATIONS*

*ROB BOTWRIGHT*

## Chapter 1: Introduction to iOS Device Forensics

Digital forensics involves the systematic collection, examination, and analysis of digital devices and data to uncover evidence and investigate incidents. It plays a crucial role in both criminal investigations and corporate environments, where understanding digital footprints is essential for uncovering malicious activities, proving wrongdoing, or reconstructing events. The process begins with identification and preservation of digital evidence, ensuring it remains unchanged during collection. Tools such as EnCase or FTK are employed for imaging and creating forensic copies, maintaining integrity and authenticity throughout. Once secured, forensic analysts use a variety of techniques to extract data, including logical and physical acquisition methods depending on the device and its state. Logical extraction involves accessing files and databases through software interfaces or utilities like Cellebrite UFED, enabling retrieval of call logs, messages, and application data crucial for investigations. Physical acquisition, on the other hand, bypasses the operating system to capture complete storage contents, requiring tools like dd for Linux or Magnet AXIOM for comprehensive imaging.

Analysis of acquired data involves examining file structures, metadata, and timestamps to establish timelines and reconstruct user activities. File carving techniques are utilized to recover deleted or fragmented files, using utilities such as Foremost or

Scalpel to identify file headers and footers amidst unallocated space. Moreover, decryption methods are employed to access encrypted files, employing tools like John the Ripper or Hashcat for password cracking or leveraging known vulnerabilities in cryptographic algorithms. Network forensics plays a pivotal role in investigating activities occurring over networks, utilizing packet sniffers like Wireshark or tcpdump to capture and analyze traffic for anomalous patterns or suspicious communications. Incident response procedures are crucial in digital forensics, involving rapid identification, containment, and mitigation of security breaches or data breaches using tools like Splunk or Security Onion to analyze logs and detect malicious activities.

In corporate environments, digital forensics supports regulatory compliance and internal investigations, ensuring data integrity and facilitating audits using tools like Magnet AXIOM Cyber or OpenText EnCase Endpoint Investigator. Mobile device forensics focuses on smartphones and tablets, using tools such as Oxygen Forensic Detective or XRY to extract data from iOS and Android devices, analyzing social media activity, GPS locations, and communication logs. Cloud forensics extends investigations to cloud-based platforms, requiring understanding of APIs and access logs for services like Amazon Web Services or Microsoft Azure, ensuring lawful access and preserving evidentiary integrity. Legal considerations are paramount in digital forensics, requiring adherence to chain of custody protocols and providing expert testimony in legal proceedings to substantiate findings and maintain forensic validity.

In summary, digital forensics is a dynamic and evolving field essential for investigating cybercrimes, fraud, and misconduct across diverse digital environments. It requires continuous adaptation to technological advancements, emerging threats, and regulatory requirements to effectively uncover evidence and support justice. Evolution of iOS forensics tools has been driven by the rapid evolution of Apple's mobile operating system, iOS, and the increasing complexity of digital investigations in response to emerging security threats and the growing ubiquity of iOS devices. Tools such as Cellebrite UFED and Magnet AXIOM have emerged as industry standards, enabling forensic examiners to extract and analyze data from iPhones, iPads, and other iOS devices. These tools leverage both logical and physical acquisition techniques to retrieve a wide range of data, from call logs and messages to photos, videos, and application data, essential for both criminal investigations and corporate incident response. Logical acquisition involves accessing the device's file system through software interfaces or specialized tools, such as the 'itunes_backup' command in Terminal, which creates a backup of an iOS device's data stored on a computer, providing forensic examiners with access to comprehensive data. Physical acquisition, on the other hand, bypasses the operating system to directly access the device's storage, capturing a bit-by-bit copy of its contents, often requiring specialized hardware like Cellebrite UFED or GrayKey, and techniques like 'checkra1n' to bypass device security measures and achieve full access to the file system, enabling comprehensive analysis.

iOS forensics tools have evolved to address challenges posed by encryption and security features implemented in newer iOS versions, such as encrypted backups and data protection mechanisms, necessitating advanced decryption capabilities. Tools like Elcomsoft iOS Forensic Toolkit offer decryption services that can break into encrypted backups by leveraging known vulnerabilities or exploiting authentication tokens acquired during the backup process, utilizing the 'Elcomsoft' command line tool to decrypt iOS backup files, providing forensic investigators with access to encrypted data. Furthermore, the evolution of iOS forensics tools has seen advancements in the analysis of iCloud data, as more users store their information in the cloud, requiring forensic examiners to understand and navigate iCloud's security measures and protocols. Tools like Oxygen Forensic Detective or XRY have been developed to extract and analyze iCloud backups, messages, photos, and other data stored in Apple's cloud service, leveraging APIs and authentication tokens to access and retrieve data, employing 'Oxygen' to extract iCloud backups and analyze their contents, providing investigators with critical evidence stored remotely.

Moreover, the evolution of iOS forensics tools has expanded to include the analysis of third-party applications and social media platforms, recognizing the significance of digital communications and social interactions in modern investigations. Tools like Magnet AXIOM Cyber and Oxygen Forensic Detective now support the extraction and analysis of data from popular messaging apps like WhatsApp, Signal, and Telegram, enabling examiners to reconstruct conversations, retrieve multimedia files, and track user activities across platforms, utilizing 'Magnet AXIOM Cyber' to parse and analyze data from messaging apps, providing forensic experts with actionable intelligence. As iOS forensics tools continue to evolve, they have also incorporated capabilities for artifact analysis, focusing on examining digital traces left behind by user interactions and system operations. Tools like BlackBag MacQuisition and Cellebrite Physical Analyzer can parse through device artifacts, such as cache files, cookies, and SQLite databases, extracting valuable information about user activity and application usage, leveraging 'BlackBag' to perform deep artifact analysis and uncover critical evidence for forensic investigations.

Furthermore, the evolution of iOS forensics tools has led to advancements in reporting and collaboration capabilities, enabling forensic examiners to generate detailed reports and collaborate with stakeholders in legal, law enforcement, and corporate settings. Tools like XRY and Oxygen Forensic Detective offer comprehensive reporting features that summarize findings, document chain of custody, and present evidence in a clear and concise manner, facilitating communication and decision-making among investigative teams and stakeholders, using 'Oxygen' to generate detailed forensic reports and securely share findings with legal teams, ensuring transparency and accuracy in forensic investigations. Additionally, the evolution of iOS forensics tools has responded to the global shift towards mobile device usage, with tools adapting to new iOS versions and hardware updates, ensuring compatibility and effectiveness in extracting and analyzing data from the latest iPhone and iPad models.

In summary, the evolution of iOS forensics tools continues to be driven by technological advancements, security challenges, and the increasing reliance on digital evidence in investigations. As iOS devices and their operating systems evolve, so too must the tools and techniques used by forensic examiners to uncover evidence, maintain forensic integrity, and support justice in a rapidly changing digital landscape.

## Chapter 2: Understanding iOS Device Architecture

Hardware components of iOS devices form the foundational elements that contribute to their functionality, reliability, and forensic significance in digital investigations. At the core of every iOS device lies the central processing unit (CPU), which drives the device's processing power and executes instructions. Apple's iOS devices typically feature custom-designed processors, such as the Apple A-series chips, renowned for their performance and efficiency. To identify the specific CPU model and its specifications, forensic examiners can utilize tools like 'system_profiler SPHardwareDataType' in Terminal, which provides detailed information about the hardware configuration of the device, including CPU details like model, speed, and architecture, crucial for understanding the device's capabilities and performance metrics. Alongside the CPU, iOS devices integrate random-access memory (RAM), essential for temporary data storage and quick access to active applications and processes. Examining RAM contents can reveal valuable volatile data, such as currently running applications, open files, and system state, utilizing tools like 'MacQuisition' to acquire a live RAM image or 'Magnet AXIOM' to analyze volatile data from iOS devices, enabling forensic analysts to capture and analyze volatile data before it is lost upon device shutdown or reboot.

Another critical hardware component in iOS devices is the NAND flash memory, which serves as the primary storage for the operating system, applications, and user data. NAND flash memory is non-volatile and stores data even when the device is powered off, making it a primary target for forensic imaging and data extraction. Tools such as 'dd' command in Terminal can be used to create a bit-by-bit forensic image of the NAND flash memory, preserving its contents for analysis and recovery, ensuring data integrity and maintaining forensic soundness throughout the process. Additionally, examining the NAND flash memory can provide insights into file system structures, deleted data remnants, and storage allocation, facilitating comprehensive forensic analysis and data recovery efforts in digital investigations.

iOS devices are also equipped with various sensors and input/output (I/O) interfaces that enhance user interaction and provide contextual data. Sensors like accelerometers, gyroscopes, and proximity sensors contribute to the device's functionality, enabling features such as motion sensing, orientation detection, and automatic screen dimming. These sensors generate sensor data logs that can be accessed and analyzed using forensic tools like 'forensic access' to retrieve data from these sensors, providing forensic examiners with information about device movements, interactions, and environmental conditions at specific times, supporting event reconstruction and user behavior analysis in investigations.

Moreover, iOS devices incorporate connectivity features such as Wi-Fi, Bluetooth, and cellular communication capabilities, enabling network access and data transmission. Examining network interfaces and connection logs using tools like 'tcpdump' or 'Wireshark' can reveal communication patterns, network activities, and interactions with external servers or devices, providing insights into online activities, messaging, and internet browsing history. Furthermore, iOS devices include biometric authentication mechanisms like Touch ID or Face ID, enhancing security and user convenience. Forensic analysis of biometric data involves extracting encrypted biometric templates stored in the Secure Enclave, using tools like 'Elcomsoft' to decrypt and analyze biometric data from iOS devices, providing forensic examiners with insights into device access and authentication events.

In addition to these components, iOS devices feature a variety of hardware-based security features designed to protect user data and maintain device integrity. The Secure Enclave, a dedicated coprocessor embedded within the device's architecture, safeguards sensitive information such as cryptographic keys and biometric data, employing sophisticated encryption and authentication mechanisms to prevent unauthorized access. The iOS operating system is structured into several layers, each playing a crucial role in its functionality, security, and interaction with applications and hardware. At the core of iOS lies the kernel, which serves as the central component responsible for managing system resources, facilitating communication between hardware and software components, and enforcing security policies. To inspect kernel details, forensic analysts can utilize tools such as 'sysdiagnose' on iOS devices, capturing diagnostic logs and kernel information that provide insights into system operations and potential security incidents, enabling comprehensive analysis and troubleshooting in forensic examinations. Above the kernel, iOS incorporates various layers that collectively manage different aspects of device operation and user interaction.

One significant layer is the Core OS layer, which includes essential system services and frameworks required for device operation. This layer manages low-level functionalities such as power management, memory allocation, and device drivers, ensuring efficient resource utilization and hardware interaction. Forensic analysis at the Core OS layer involves examining system logs and configuration files using commands like 'log show' in Terminal, retrieving information about system events, error messages, and system state changes that may be relevant to investigations, enabling forensic experts to reconstruct device activities and identify potential security breaches.

Above the Core OS layer, iOS includes the Core Services layer, which provides fundamental services and APIs for application development and system-level functionalities. This layer encompasses services such as iCloud synchronization, authentication mechanisms, and data management frameworks, supporting seamless integration of applications and services across iOS devices. Forensic analysis at the Core Services layer involves examining application data stored in iCloud using tools like 'icloud access' to retrieve and analyze synchronized data, such as photos, documents, and application backups stored in Apple's cloud service, facilitating comprehensive examination of digital evidence in investigations.

Further up the iOS operating system stack is the Media layer, which manages multimedia processing and playback functionalities on iOS devices. This layer includes frameworks for handling audio, video, and image data, supporting multimedia applications and content consumption experiences. Forensic examination at the Media layer involves analyzing media files and metadata using tools like 'mediainfo' to extract information about file properties, codecs, and creation timestamps, providing forensic examiners with insights into media consumption patterns, file origins, and potential tampering in investigations.

Above the Media layer, iOS incorporates the Cocoa Touch layer, which encompasses user interface frameworks and application development libraries tailored for iOS applications. This layer enables the creation of intuitive and responsive user interfaces, incorporating touch-based interactions, gestures, and animations that define the user experience on iOS devices. Forensic analysis at the Cocoa Touch layer involves examining application artifacts, such as user interface elements and interaction logs, using tools like 'UI inspector' to inspect application interfaces and capture user interaction details, enabling forensic experts to reconstruct user activities and interactions with applications in forensic investigations. At the highest layer of the iOS operating system stack is the Application layer, which comprises user-installed applications and system-provided apps that deliver various functionalities and services to iOS device users. This layer includes applications such as Messages, Safari, Mail, and third-party apps downloaded from the App Store, catering to diverse user needs ranging from communication and productivity to entertainment and social networking. Forensic analysis at the Application layer involves examining application data stored locally on the device using tools like 'forensic access' to retrieve data from applications' storage areas, including databases, preferences, and caches, facilitating comprehensive analysis of application usage patterns, communication histories, and stored content in forensic investigations.

Throughout these layers, iOS incorporates robust security mechanisms and privacy controls designed to protect user data and ensure secure operation of the device and applications. Security features such as data encryption, sandboxing, and secure boot ensure data confidentiality, integrity, and device authenticity, safeguarding against unauthorized access and malicious activities. Forensic analysis of iOS security features involves examining security-related configurations and audit logs using tools like 'security audit' to detect security incidents, access control violations, and system compromises, enabling forensic experts to assess the effectiveness of security measures and identify potential vulnerabilities in forensic examinations.

In summary, the layered architecture of the iOS operating system encompasses essential components and functionalities that collectively contribute to its reliability, security, and user experience on Apple's mobile devices. Forensic analysis at each layer provides forensic examiners with valuable insights into device operations, user interactions, and digital evidence stored on iOS devices, enabling comprehensive investigations, incident response, and legal proceedings in a rapidly evolving digital landscape.

# Chapter 3: Basics of Data Acquisition from iOS Devices

Physical and logical acquisition are two fundamental approaches in digital forensics for extracting data from electronic devices, each serving distinct purposes and offering unique advantages depending on the investigation's requirements and the device's state. Physical acquisition involves obtaining a bit-by-bit copy of the device's storage media, capturing everything stored on the device, including active and deleted data, system files, and application data. The process typically requires specialized tools and hardware capable of bypassing device security measures and accessing low-level storage areas, such as using tools like 'dd' command in Terminal to create a forensic image of the entire storage of a device, ensuring a complete and accurate copy of the data for forensic analysis. This approach is particularly useful in cases where comprehensive data recovery is necessary, such as retrieving deleted files or uncovering hidden data that may not be accessible through other means.

On the other hand, logical acquisition focuses on extracting specific data sets from the device's file system and databases using software interfaces or protocols supported by the operating system. This method targets accessible data areas without accessing the entire storage medium, making it faster and less intrusive compared to physical acquisition. Forensic examiners can deploy logical acquisition techniques using tools like 'iTunes' to create a backup of an iOS device or 'adb' command for Android devices to retrieve application data, messages, call logs, and other user-generated content stored in accessible areas, enabling targeted data extraction while preserving device integrity and reducing the risk of altering evidentiary data.

The choice between physical and logical acquisition depends on various factors, including the device's security settings, the investigation's scope, and the type of data required for analysis. Physical acquisition is preferred when dealing with locked or encrypted devices, as it bypasses security measures and provides access to all data stored on the device, including encrypted and deleted files that may be crucial for forensic examinations. Tools like 'GrayKey' for iOS or 'Cellebrite UFED' for Android are commonly used by forensic professionals to bypass device locks and extract complete data images, ensuring comprehensive analysis and evidence preservation in legal proceedings.

Conversely, logical acquisition is suitable for scenarios where direct access to the device's storage is limited or restricted, such as when dealing with devices protected by strong encryption or cloud synchronization services. By utilizing software-based extraction methods and protocols supported by the device's operating system, forensic examiners can retrieve valuable user data without altering the device's state or triggering security alerts, ensuring forensic soundness and preserving evidentiary integrity throughout the investigation process. Techniques such as 'adb backup' for Android devices or 'iTunes backup' for iOS devices enable forensic analysts to create backups of device data, including application data, photos, and messages, facilitating detailed analysis and reconstruction of digital activities in forensic investigations.

Moreover, physical and logical acquisition methods complement each other in digital forensics, allowing forensic examiners to apply a comprehensive approach to data collection and analysis based on the specific requirements of each case. Physical acquisition provides a complete view of the device's storage, offering insights into hidden or protected data that may not be accessible through logical means alone. By contrast, logical acquisition offers a targeted approach to retrieving specific data sets quickly and efficiently, focusing on user-generated content and application data stored in accessible areas of the device's file system.

In practice, forensic professionals often combine physical and logical acquisition techniques to maximize data recovery and analysis capabilities while adhering to legal and ethical standards governing digital evidence handling. This hybrid approach enables examiners to obtain a comprehensive view of device contents while preserving evidentiary integrity and ensuring compliance with chain of custody protocols. By leveraging both methods strategically, forensic analysts can uncover critical evidence, reconstruct digital timelines, and provide actionable insights that support investigative efforts and facilitate informed decision-making in legal proceedings.

Overall, the distinction between physical and logical acquisition underscores the importance of selecting the appropriate method based on the specific circumstances of each forensic investigation, balancing the need for comprehensive data recovery with the requirements for maintaining forensic integrity and adherence to legal standards. As digital devices evolve and security measures advance, forensic professionals continue to refine their techniques and adopt innovative tools to effectively navigate challenges and uncover crucial evidence in increasingly complex digital environmentsExtraction methods and tools play a critical role in digital forensics, enabling investigators to retrieve and analyze data from electronic devices while maintaining forensic integrity and adhering to legal standards. One of the primary extraction methods used in digital forensics is logical acquisition, which involves retrieving specific data sets from a device's file system and databases through software interfaces or protocols supported by the operating system. For iOS devices, logical acquisition often begins with creating a backup using the 'iTunes' application, which stores a snapshot of the device's data on a computer, allowing forensic examiners to access files such as messages, call logs, and application data crucial for investigations. Similarly, Android devices utilize the 'adb backup' command in

Terminal to create backups that can be analyzed using forensic tools like 'Autopsy' or 'Magnet AXIOM', providing examiners with insights into user activities and stored content.

In contrast to logical acquisition, physical acquisition involves obtaining a bit-by-bit copy of the device's storage media, capturing everything stored on the device including active and deleted data, system files, and application data. This method requires specialized tools and hardware capable of bypassing device security measures and accessing low-level storage areas. Tools like 'dd' command in Terminal are commonly used to create a forensic image of the entire storage of a device, ensuring a complete and accurate copy of the data for forensic analysis. Physical acquisition is particularly valuable in cases where comprehensive data recovery is necessary, such as retrieving deleted files or uncovering hidden data that may not be accessible through other means.

For iOS devices specifically, physical acquisition tools such as 'Cellebrite UFED' or 'GrayKey' are widely used by forensic professionals to bypass device locks and extract complete data images. These tools employ proprietary techniques to exploit vulnerabilities or weaknesses in iOS security measures, enabling examiners to access encrypted or deleted data that may be critical to investigations. Similarly, Android devices can be analyzed using physical acquisition tools like 'Magnet AXIOM' or 'XRY', which provide capabilities to bypass device locks and retrieve comprehensive data images for forensic analysis, ensuring forensic soundness and preserving evidentiary integrity throughout the investigation process.

Beyond traditional extraction methods, cloud forensics has emerged as a crucial area of focus in digital investigations, enabling examiners to retrieve and analyze data stored in cloud-based services such as iCloud, Google Drive, or Dropbox. Cloud extraction tools like 'Elcomsoft Phone Breaker' or 'Oxygen Forensic Detective' facilitate access to synchronized data, backups, and application files stored in remote servers, leveraging authentication tokens and APIs to retrieve information relevant to investigations. This approach is essential for examining digital footprints left across multiple platforms and devices, providing examiners with a comprehensive view of user activities and communications conducted through cloud services.

Moreover, data carving techniques are employed in digital forensics to recover fragmented or deleted files from storage media, reconstructing files based on file headers, footers, and data patterns. Tools like 'Scalpel' or 'Foremost' are used to identify and extract file fragments from unallocated disk space or damaged storage media, enabling examiners to recover deleted documents, images, or other file types that may contain critical evidence for investigations. Data carving is particularly valuable in cases where files have been intentionally deleted or damaged to conceal incriminating information, allowing forensic analysts to reconstruct digital artifacts and reconstruct the timeline of events.

In addition to extraction methods, forensic examiners utilize a range of analysis tools and techniques to interpret and examine extracted data in detail. Data analysis tools such as 'Autopsy', 'Encase', or 'Magnet AXIOM' provide capabilities to parse, search, and visualize data from forensic images or acquired backups, facilitating keyword searches, timeline reconstruction, and correlation of digital artifacts across multiple sources. These tools enable examiners to identify patterns, connections, and anomalies within the extracted data, supporting investigative efforts and generating actionable insights for legal proceedings.

Furthermore, mobile device management (MDM) solutions play a crucial role in enterprise environments by providing centralized control over device configurations, applications, and data access policies. MDM tools like 'Jamf', 'MobileIron', or 'Microsoft Intune' enable organizations to remotely manage and monitor iOS and Android devices, enforce security policies, and facilitate data retrieval or device wipe operations in response to security incidents or compliance requirements. In forensic investigations, MDM solutions can be leveraged to retrieve device information, application logs, or user activity data stored in enterprise environments, providing additional context and insights into device usage and policy compliance.

Overall, extraction methods and tools continue to evolve in response to technological advancements, security challenges, and the increasing reliance on digital evidence in investigations. Forensic professionals must stay abreast of new developments and techniques to effectively navigate complex digital landscapes, ensuring thorough and legally sound investigations that uphold the integrity of digital evidence. By leveraging a combination of logical, physical, and cloud extraction methods alongside advanced analysis tools, forensic examiners can uncover critical evidence, reconstruct digital timelines, and provide valuable insights that support investigative efforts and contribute to justice.

# Chapter 4: iOS File System Analysis

The structure of the iOS file system is meticulously organized to ensure efficient operation, data security, and seamless integration of applications and user data across Apple's mobile devices. At the core of the iOS file system is the root directory (/), which serves as the starting point for navigating through the entire file hierarchy. To explore the file system structure in detail, forensic analysts can use commands such as 'ls' in Terminal, which lists directory contents, providing a comprehensive view of files, folders, and symbolic links present within each directory. Within the root directory, essential system directories such as /System and /Library house critical system files, frameworks, and configuration settings that govern the device's operation and support core functionalities.

One of the distinctive features of the iOS file system is its use of a secure sandboxing mechanism, which isolates each application's data and resources within its designated sandbox directory (/var/mobile/Applications). This ensures that applications cannot access data from other applications or system files, enhancing security and protecting user privacy. Forensic examination of application sandboxes involves navigating through individual directories using commands like 'cd' in Terminal, accessing application-specific data such as documents, caches, and preferences stored within each sandbox, enabling forensic examiners to analyze application usage patterns, stored content, and user interactions in investigations.

The iOS file system also incorporates a unified data storage model, known as the Media folder (/var/mobile/Media), which serves as a central repository for user-generated content, including photos, videos, music, and downloaded files. This folder structure facilitates seamless synchronization and access to multimedia content across iOS devices and cloud services, enabling users to manage and share their digital assets effortlessly. In forensic investigations, examining the Media folder involves navigating through subdirectories using commands like 'ls -l' to display detailed file information, retrieving multimedia files and metadata stored within the directory structure, providing examiners with insights into user media consumption and content creation activities.

Moreover, iOS devices utilize a proprietary file system called Apple File System (APFS), which replaced the earlier Hierarchical File System Plus (HFS+) with enhanced features optimized for modern storage technologies and security requirements. APFS supports advanced storage features such as snapshots, encryption, and space sharing, improving data integrity, performance, and reliability across iOS devices. To analyze an iOS device formatted with APFS, forensic analysts can use tools like 'diskutil' command in Terminal to list APFS volumes and partitions, examining volume structures and properties to understand data organization and storage allocation within the file system.

Within the APFS file system, each volume contains containers that store multiple volumes, facilitating flexible management of storage space and data allocation across different partitions. The container directory structure can be explored using commands like 'diskutil apfs list' to display container and volume details, identifying primary and secondary volumes within the APFS container, facilitating forensic analysis and data extraction from specific volumes based on investigative requirements. Additionally, APFS supports native encryption capabilities, enabling data protection through file-level encryption and secure metadata handling, ensuring confidentiality and integrity of user data stored on iOS devices.

Furthermore, the iOS file system includes directories dedicated to system logs and diagnostic information, essential for monitoring device performance, troubleshooting issues, and capturing forensic evidence in investigations. Directories such as /private/var/log store system log files generated by various subsystems and applications, recording events, errors, and system state changes over time. Forensic analysis of system logs involves accessing log files using commands like 'cat' or 'grep' in Terminal, searching for specific keywords or patterns to identify anomalous activities, security incidents, or unauthorized access attempts recorded in system logs, providing examiners with valuable insights into device usage and operational events.

In addition to system directories, iOS devices maintain directories for storing temporary files, caches, and application data, optimizing performance and enhancing user experience. The /private/var/mobile/Library/Caches directory, for example, stores application-specific cache files used to temporarily store data for quick access and retrieval by applications, improving responsiveness and efficiency. Forensic examination of cache directories involves accessing cache files using commands like 'find' in Terminal, identifying cached data related to specific applications or user activities stored within cache directories, facilitating analysis of application usage patterns and data interactions in forensic investigations.

Overall, the structured design of the iOS file system reflects Apple's commitment to data security, system performance, and user privacy, incorporating advanced storage technologies and security features to safeguard user data and support seamless data management across iOS devices. Forensic analysts leverage command-line tools, terminal commands, and specialized forensic software to navigate, explore, and extract data from the iOS file system, ensuring thorough analysis and preservation of digital evidence in investigations. By understanding the intricacies of the iOS file system structure and its components, forensic professionals can effectively uncover critical evidence, reconstruct digital timelines, and provide actionable insights that support investigative efforts and legal proceedings in a dynamic digital landscape. File metadata and attributes constitute essential components in digital forensics, providing valuable information about files, their characteristics, and their history within a file system. Metadata includes descriptive data that describe various aspects of a file, such as creation date, modification timestamps, file size, and permissions, facilitating forensic analysis and reconstruction of digital artifacts. To examine file metadata in Unix-based systems like macOS or Linux, forensic analysts can use commands such as 'stat' in Terminal, which retrieves detailed information about file attributes, including access times, inode numbers, and file ownership, enabling comprehensive analysis of file properties and system interactions in forensic investigations.

Attributes associated with files include flags and settings that define their behavior and accessibility within the file system. For instance, file attributes such as 'immutable' or 'append-only' can be set using commands like 'chflags' in Terminal to restrict modifications or prevent deletion of critical files, enhancing data integrity and preserving forensic evidence in secure environments. By examining file attributes using commands like 'ls -l' or 'lsattr', forensic examiners can identify special flags and settings applied to files or directories, assessing their impact on data security, access controls, and integrity verification in forensic examinations.

File metadata also encompasses extended attributes (xattrs), which store additional information beyond standard file attributes, such as file tags, metadata tags, or custom user-defined attributes. To view extended attributes associated with a file in macOS or Linux, forensic analysts can use commands like 'xattr -l' in Terminal, displaying a list of extended attributes and their corresponding values, providing insights into file origin, usage context, or application-specific metadata stored within files. Examining extended attributes is crucial for identifying hidden data, forensic artifacts, or metadata tags that may be relevant to investigations, enabling examiners to reconstruct digital activities and validate data integrity in forensic examinations.

In addition to standard metadata and extended attributes, file systems often maintain journaling mechanisms that record changes made to files and directories over time, enhancing data consistency and recovery capabilities in the event of system failures or unexpected shutdowns. Journaling file systems such as HFS+ (Hierarchical File System Plus) or APFS (Apple File System) maintain transaction logs containing metadata updates and file system operations, enabling forensic analysts to review journal entries using commands like 'fs_usage' or 'journalctl' in Terminal, identifying file system events, access patterns, and user interactions recorded in journal logs, facilitating reconstruction of digital timelines and event sequences in forensic investigations.

Moreover, forensic analysis of file metadata extends to examining file system structures and data allocation mechanisms used to organize and manage storage space within the file system. File systems like APFS utilize B-trees and space allocation maps to manage file storage and optimize data access, supporting features such as copy-on-write snapshots, space sharing, and efficient file system operations. To analyze file system structures and allocation details, forensic examiners can use commands like 'diskutil apfs list' in Terminal, displaying APFS container and volume information, examining volume properties, and identifying data allocation patterns within the file system, enabling comprehensive analysis of storage usage and data allocation strategies in forensic examinations.

Furthermore, file metadata plays a crucial role in digital investigations involving data recovery and forensic analysis of deleted or overwritten files. Deleted file recovery tools such as 'PhotoRec' or 'TestDisk' utilize file metadata and data carving techniques to reconstruct deleted files from unallocated disk space or damaged storage media, identifying file headers, footers, and data signatures to recover fragmented or partially overwritten data. By examining metadata attributes such as deletion timestamps or file status indicators, forensic examiners can determine the presence of deleted files, assess their recoverability, and reconstruct digital artifacts associated with user activities or system events in forensic examinations.

In forensic investigations, file metadata and attributes serve as vital sources of information for reconstructing digital activities, validating evidence integrity, and establishing timelines of events based on file system interactions and data modifications. By leveraging command-line tools, terminal commands, and specialized forensic software, forensic professionals can navigate, analyze, and interpret file metadata effectively, ensuring thorough examination and preservation of digital evidence in compliance with legal and regulatory requirements. Understanding the nuances of file metadata and attributes enables examiners to uncover critical evidence, identify data anomalies, and provide actionable insights that support investigative efforts and contribute to the resolution of legal proceedings in digital forensics.

## Chapter 5: Introduction to iCloud Forensics

iCloud storage and synchronization constitute integral components of Apple's ecosystem, enabling seamless access, backup, and synchronization of user data across iOS devices, Mac computers, and Windows PCs. iCloud serves as a cloud-based storage solution that facilitates the secure storage of photos, videos, documents, application data, and device backups, enhancing user convenience and data accessibility. To manage iCloud storage and synchronization settings on iOS devices, users can navigate to 'Settings' > '[User's Name]' > 'iCloud' to configure options for enabling iCloud backup, synchronizing data across devices, and managing storage usage. Additionally, iCloud synchronization settings can be managed using the 'icloudctl' command-line tool in Terminal, enabling administrators to monitor and control iCloud synchronization activitles, including file uploads, downloads, and data transfers between devices and iCloud servers, ensuring data integrity and compliance with organizational policies.

The synchronization process in iCloud relies on Apple's proprietary synchronization protocols and encryption mechanisms, ensuring data security and privacy protection during data transmission and storage. iCloud uses end-to-end encryption to secure user data in transit and at rest, utilizing protocols such as HTTPS, TLS, and AES encryption to protect data integrity and confidentiality. Forensic analysis of iCloud synchronization involves examining synchronization logs and metadata using commands like 'icloudpd' or 'icloud-sync', retrieving metadata information, and analyzing synchronization activities between devices and iCloud servers to reconstruct digital activities, user interactions, and data transfers in forensic investigations.

Furthermore, iCloud storage offers automatic synchronization of application data, including calendars, contacts, notes, and reminders, across devices connected to the same iCloud account. To synchronize application data on iOS devices, users can enable iCloud synchronization settings for individual applications, ensuring consistency and real-time updates across devices. Command-line tools like 'icloudpd sync' or 'icloud-sync -a' enable forensic examiners to synchronize application data and retrieve synchronized files stored in iCloud, facilitating analysis of application usage patterns, data interactions, and synchronization activities in forensic examinations.

In addition to application data synchronization, iCloud facilitates automatic backup of iOS devices, enabling users to create secure backups of device settings, application data, photos, videos, and other user-generated content. iCloud backups are encrypted and stored in the user's iCloud account, accessible for restoration and recovery purposes in case of device loss, damage, or data corruption. To manage iCloud backups on iOS devices, users can navigate to 'Settings'

> '[User's Name]' > 'iCloud' > 'iCloud Backup' to enable automatic backups, manage backup settings, and view backup status. Command-line tools like 'icloudpd backup' or 'icloud-backup -m' enable forensic analysts to retrieve iCloud backups, decrypt backup files, and extract stored data for forensic analysis, enabling examiners to recover deleted files, analyze application data, and reconstruct digital artifacts in forensic investigations.

Moreover, iCloud storage supports synchronization of multimedia content, including photos, videos, and music, across iOS devices and integrated applications such as Photos and iCloud Music Library. By enabling iCloud Photo Library or iCloud Music Library, users can synchronize multimedia content across devices, ensuring access to media files and personalized playlists from any connected device. Command-line tools like 'icloudpd photos' or 'icloud-sync -p' enable forensic examiners to retrieve synchronized photos and videos stored in iCloud, analyzing metadata, EXIF data, and geolocation information associated with multimedia files to reconstruct digital timelines, user activities, and media consumption patterns in forensic investigations.

Additionally, iCloud Drive serves as a file storage and synchronization service, enabling users to store documents, presentations, spreadsheets, and other file types in iCloud and access them from any iOS device, Mac computer, or Windows PC. To manage iCloud Drive settings and synchronize files across devices, users can access iCloud Drive through the Files app on iOS devices or Finder on Mac computers, organizing files into folders and enabling automatic synchronization using commands like 'icloudctl sync' or 'icloud-sync -f' in Terminal. Forensic analysis of iCloud Drive involves examining file metadata, access logs, and synchronization activities, identifying file modifications, access patterns, and user interactions recorded in iCloud Drive, facilitating reconstruction of file histories, document workflows, and collaborative activities in forensic examinations.

Furthermore, iCloud Keychain provides secure storage and synchronization of passwords, account credentials, and sensitive information across devices, enhancing convenience and security for users accessing websites, apps, and services. Command-line tools like 'icloudpd keychain' or 'icloud-sync -k' enable forensic analysts to retrieve synchronized keychain data stored in iCloud, examining saved passwords, secure notes, and authentication tokens associated with user accounts, facilitating analysis of credential usage, login activities, and access patterns in forensic investigations.

In summary, iCloud storage and synchronization play a crucial role in Apple's ecosystem, enabling seamless data management, backup, and synchronization across iOS devices, Mac computers, and Windows PCs. By leveraging command-line tools, terminal commands, and specialized forensic software, forensic professionals can navigate, analyze, and interpret iCloud synchronization activities and stored data effectively, ensuring thorough examination and preservation of digital evidence in compliance with legal and regulatory standards. Understanding the intricacies of iCloud storage and synchronization enables examiners to uncover critical evidence, reconstruct digital activities, and provide actionable insights that support investigative efforts and contribute to the resolution of legal proceedings in digital forensics. Forensic examination of iCloud data presents unique challenges and complexities due to Apple's stringent security measures, encryption protocols, and synchronization mechanisms designed to protect user privacy and data integrity. iCloud data, including backups, synchronized content, and application data, is encrypted both in transit and at rest using strong cryptographic algorithms and protocols such as HTTPS, TLS, and AES encryption, ensuring that data remains secure and confidential during transmission between devices and iCloud servers. This encryption presents a significant challenge for forensic examiners seeking to access and analyze iCloud data, as decryption requires access to encryption keys stored securely by Apple and authorization from the account holder to retrieve encrypted data stored in iCloud.

One of the primary challenges in forensic examination of iCloud data is obtaining lawful access and authorization to retrieve encrypted content stored in iCloud accounts. Apple employs end-to-end encryption for iCloud data, meaning that only the account holder possesses the encryption keys necessary to decrypt and access their stored data. Forensic examiners may encounter legal and procedural hurdles in obtaining access to encryption keys or compelling Apple to provide access to encrypted iCloud data, as Apple prioritizes user privacy and data protection in compliance with legal requirements and privacy regulations.

Another challenge in forensic analysis of iCloud data is the synchronization and deletion mechanisms implemented by Apple, which may impact data availability and retention periods for synchronized content and backups. iCloud synchronization processes automatically upload and synchronize user data across devices connected to the same iCloud account, including photos, videos, documents, and application data. However, deleted data or files may be retained in iCloud backups or synchronization history, posing challenges for forensic examiners attempting to recover and analyze deleted or overwritten data from iCloud storage. Tools like 'icloudpd' or 'icloud-sync' enable forensic analysts to retrieve synchronized data and backups stored in iCloud, examining metadata, file attributes, and synchronization logs to reconstruct digital activities and recover deleted files in forensic investigations.

Furthermore, forensic analysis of iCloud backups presents challenges related to data extraction, decryption, and validation of backup integrity. iCloud backups are encrypted and stored securely in the user's iCloud account, accessible for restoration and recovery purposes but requiring decryption to access and analyze backup contents. Tools like 'icloudpd backup' or 'icloud-backup -d' enable forensic examiners to download and decrypt iCloud backups, retrieving stored data, application settings, and device configurations for forensic analysis. However, decryption of iCloud backups may be subject to legal constraints and technical limitations, as forensic examiners must adhere to legal requirements and obtain appropriate authorization to access encrypted backup contents stored in iCloud.

Moreover, the dynamic nature of iCloud synchronization and data retention policies poses challenges for forensic examiners seeking to reconstruct digital timelines and establish data integrity in iCloud investigations. iCloud synchronization processes continuously update and synchronize user data across devices, reflecting real-time changes and modifications made to synchronized content such as photos, videos, and documents. Command-line tools like 'icloudctl sync' or 'icloud-sync -u' enable forensic analysts to monitor synchronization activities, retrieve updated data, and analyze metadata changes recorded in iCloud synchronization logs, facilitating reconstruction of digital interactions and user activities across multiple devices in forensic examinations.

Additionally, forensic examiners must consider the impact of Apple's security updates, software patches, and system upgrades on iCloud data accessibility and forensic analysis. Apple regularly updates iCloud security measures and encryption protocols to address emerging threats and vulnerabilities, enhancing data protection and privacy for iCloud users. However, these updates may introduce changes to encryption algorithms, data storage formats, or synchronization mechanisms, requiring forensic analysts to adapt forensic tools and techniques to maintain compatibility and effectiveness in analyzing iCloud data across different iOS and macOS versions.

Furthermore, legal and jurisdictional considerations play a crucial role in forensic examinations of iCloud data, as international privacy laws and regulations may impose restrictions on accessing, retrieving, and transferring iCloud data across borders. Forensic examiners must comply with legal requirements, obtain appropriate legal authorization, and adhere to lawful processes when accessing iCloud data stored in different jurisdictions, ensuring compliance with data protection regulations and safeguarding user privacy rights in forensic investigations.

In summary, forensic examination of iCloud data presents multifaceted challenges related to encryption, synchronization mechanisms, data retention policies, legal compliance, and jurisdictional considerations. By leveraging command-line tools, terminal commands, and specialized forensic software, forensic professionals can navigate these challenges effectively, ensuring thorough analysis and preservation of digital evidence in compliance with legal and regulatory standards. Understanding the complexities of iCloud data forensic challenges enables examiners to develop comprehensive strategies, overcome technical and legal hurdles, and provide actionable insights that support investigative efforts and contribute to the resolution of legal proceedings in digital forensics

## Chapter 6: Securing and Handling Digital Evidence

Effective evidence collection is paramount in digital forensics, ensuring the preservation, integrity, and admissibility of digital evidence in legal proceedings and investigative processes. Adopting best practices in evidence collection involves meticulous planning, adherence to standardized procedures, and utilization of specialized tools and techniques to capture, document, and analyze digital artifacts from various sources, including computers, mobile devices, and cloud services. Forensic examiners follow established protocols and guidelines to mitigate the risk of data contamination, alteration, or loss during evidence collection, employing command-line tools such as 'dd' to create forensic disk images of storage media, preserving a bit-by-bit copy of digital evidence while maintaining data integrity and authenticity.

Maintaining chain of custody is a critical aspect of evidence collection, documenting the handling, transfer, and storage of digital evidence throughout the forensic investigation process. Forensic examiners use command-line tools like 'md5sum' or 'sha256sum' to calculate hash values of forensic disk images and digital artifacts, generating unique cryptographic identifiers that serve as digital fingerprints to verify data integrity and detect unauthorized alterations or tampering. By documenting chain of custody procedures and maintaining detailed records of evidence handling, examiners establish accountability, traceability, and reliability of digital evidence presented in court or during investigative proceedings.

Furthermore, forensic examiners employ live forensics techniques to collect volatile data and system artifacts from running operating systems and active processes, facilitating real-time analysis and preservation of digital evidence in forensic investigations. Command-line tools such as 'ps' and 'netstat' enable examiners to list active processes and network connections, capturing volatile data such as running applications, open files, and network activities that may provide insights into user activities, system configurations, and potential security incidents. Live forensics enables examiners to acquire time-sensitive data, identify malicious activities, and respond promptly to security breaches or digital incidents affecting computer systems and network environments.

In addition to live forensics, forensic examiners conduct acquisition of non-volatile data from storage media using write-blocking hardware or software tools to prevent inadvertent modification of digital evidence during data acquisition. Command-line tools such as 'dcfldd' or 'foremost' facilitate targeted data recovery and extraction from storage devices, enabling examiners to recover deleted files, carve data fragments, and reconstruct digital artifacts from damaged or corrupted storage media in forensic examinations. By employing write-blocking mechanisms and using validated forensic tools, examiners preserve data integrity and ensure admissibility of digital evidence in legal proceedings.

Moreover, forensic examiners employ network forensics techniques to capture, analyze, and reconstruct digital evidence from network communications, including packet captures, log files, and network traffic data. Command-line tools such as 'tcpdump' or 'Wireshark' enable examiners to capture network packets, filter traffic based on protocol or IP address, and analyze communication patterns, identifying malicious activities, unauthorized access attempts, or data exfiltration incidents occurring over network channels. Network forensics provides insights into network-based attacks, intrusion attempts, and unauthorized access incidents, enabling examiners to attribute digital evidence to specific network events and entities involved in forensic investigations.

Additionally, forensic examiners conduct memory forensics to analyze volatile memory (RAM) contents and identify active processes, malware artifacts, and system configurations present in memory at the time of data acquisition. Command-line tools such as 'Volatility' or 'Rekall' facilitate memory dump analysis, enabling examiners to extract process memory, analyze memory structures, and identify malicious code or unauthorized activities occurring in memory. Memory forensics provides valuable insights into system compromises, rootkit installations, and memory-resident malware infections, facilitating incident response efforts and forensic investigations aimed at identifying and mitigating cyber threats.

Furthermore, forensic examiners utilize mobile device forensics techniques to collect, analyze, and extract digital evidence from smartphones, tablets, and wearable devices running iOS, Android, or other mobile operating systems. Command-line tools such as 'adb' (Android Debug Bridge) or 'ideviceinfo' enable examiners to access device information, retrieve device logs, and perform data acquisition from mobile devices, including call logs, SMS messages, photos, and application data. Mobile device forensics encompasses physical and logical acquisition methods, enabling examiners to recover deleted data, analyze application artifacts, and reconstruct user activities stored on mobile devices in forensic investigations.

In summary, adopting best practices in evidence collection is essential for ensuring the integrity, authenticity, and admissibility of digital evidence in forensic investigations and legal proceedings. By following standardized procedures, leveraging command-line tools, and employing specialized forensic techniques, examiners can effectively capture, document, and analyze digital artifacts from diverse sources, including computers, mobile devices, and network environments. Effective evidence collection enhances the credibility and reliability of digital evidence presented in court, supporting investigative efforts and contributing to the resolution of criminal cases, civil disputes, and cybersecurity incidents in digital forensics. Chain of custody procedures in digital forensics are critical protocols designed to maintain the integrity, reliability, and admissibility of digital evidence throughout the investigative process and in legal proceedings. These procedures involve documenting the handling, transfer, and storage of digital evidence from the initial collection phase to its presentation in court, ensuring accountability, transparency, and preservation of evidentiary value. Forensic examiners meticulously follow established chain of custody guidelines, utilizing command-line tools such as 'md5sum' or 'sha256sum' to calculate cryptographic hash values of digital artifacts, generating unique identifiers that serve as digital fingerprints to verify data integrity and detect unauthorized alterations or tampering.

The chain of custody process begins with the identification and documentation of digital evidence at the crime scene or incident location, where forensic examiners use tools like 'foremost' or 'dcfldd' to perform on-site data acquisition, creating forensic disk images of storage media to preserve a bit-by-bit copy of digital evidence while preventing accidental modifications or data loss. By employing write-blocking hardware or software tools during data acquisition, examiners ensure that original evidence remains intact and unaltered, maintaining chain of custody integrity and compliance with forensic standards and legal requirements.

Once digital evidence is collected, forensic examiners establish initial chain of custody documentation, recording pertinent details such as date, time, location, and individuals involved in evidence collection, using standardized forms or electronic records management systems to document chain of custody entries and updates throughout the investigative process. Command-line tools like 'grep' or 'awk' enable examiners to search and analyze chain of custody logs, identifying entries, timestamps, and custody transfers recorded during evidence handling and storage procedures, facilitating accountability and traceability of digital evidence presented in legal proceedings.

Moreover, chain of custody procedures include secure storage and preservation of digital evidence in controlled environments, such as forensic laboratories or evidence lockers equipped with physical and cybersecurity measures to prevent unauthorized access, tampering, or data breaches. Forensic examiners use command-line tools like 'chmod' or 'chown' to set file permissions and access controls, restricting access to digital evidence files and directories based on role-based permissions and security policies, ensuring data confidentiality and integrity throughout the chain of custody lifecycle.

In addition to physical security measures, chain of custody procedures encompass digital security practices to protect against cyber threats, data breaches, or unauthorized modifications of digital evidence stored in forensic repositories or cloud-based storage solutions. Command-line tools such as 'gpg' (GNU Privacy Guard) or 'openssl' enable examiners to encrypt digital evidence files and containers, implementing strong encryption algorithms like AES-256 to safeguard sensitive data during storage, transit, and archival processes, ensuring compliance with data protection regulations and cybersecurity best practices in digital forensics.

Furthermore, chain of custody documentation includes periodic audits and verifications conducted by forensic supervisors or independent auditors to validate the accuracy, completeness, and consistency of chain of custody records, ensuring adherence to forensic protocols and regulatory requirements governing evidence handling and storage practices. Command-line tools like 'diff' or 'rsync' facilitate file and directory comparisons, enabling examiners to detect discrepancies or unauthorized changes in chain of custody logs, enhancing transparency and accountability of digital evidence management in forensic investigations.

Additionally, chain of custody procedures extend to evidence presentation and courtroom testimony, where forensic examiners provide detailed chain of custody reports, affidavits, or deposition statements to authenticate digital evidence and validate its admissibility in legal proceedings. Command-line tools such as 'pdftk' or 'imagemagick' enable examiners to convert, format, and annotate digital evidence files for courtroom presentations, creating exhibits or visual aids that support investigative findings and corroborate chain of custody documentation presented to judges, juries, or legal counsel.

Moreover, chain of custody procedures emphasize the importance of continuous training, education, and professional development for forensic examiners, ensuring proficiency in current forensic methodologies, technological advancements, and legal frameworks governing chain of custody practices. Command-line tools like 'man' or 'info' enable examiners to access and review documentation, manuals, and guides on forensic procedures, best practices, and industry standards, enhancing competence and adherence to chain of custody protocols in digital forensics.

In summary, chain of custody procedures in digital forensics play a crucial role in preserving the integrity, reliability, and admissibility of digital evidence throughout the investigative process and in legal proceedings. By following established protocols, employing command-line tools, and implementing secure data handling practices, forensic examiners ensure accountability, transparency, and compliance with forensic standards, safeguarding the evidentiary value and credibility of digital evidence presented in courtrooms worldwide

## Chapter 7: Legal and Ethical Considerations in iOS Forensics

Laws governing digital evidence encompass a complex legal framework that regulates the collection, admissibility, and use of digital artifacts in legal proceedings, ensuring fairness, reliability, and integrity in the judicial process. In the United States, the Federal Rules of Evidence (FRE) and individual state rules govern the admissibility of digital evidence, emphasizing authentication, relevance, and reliability criteria to determine the probative value of digital artifacts presented in court. Command-line tools such as 'grep' or 'awk' facilitate search and analysis of legal statutes, enabling legal professionals and forensic examiners to identify relevant laws, rules, and regulations governing digital evidence admissibility and courtroom procedures.

Internationally, legal frameworks such as the European Union's General Data Protection Regulation (GDPR) and the Council of Europe's Convention on Cybercrime (Budapest Convention) establish data protection principles, privacy rights, and procedural safeguards for handling digital evidence across borders, ensuring compliance with international standards and human rights protections in cybercrime investigations. By adhering to GDPR requirements and obtaining lawful authority, forensic examiners can use commands like 'rsync' or 'scp' to securely transfer digital evidence between jurisdictions, preserving chain of custody and data integrity while respecting privacy rights and legal frameworks governing cross-border data transfers.

Furthermore, laws governing digital evidence address the admissibility of electronic communications, social media posts, and digital records in civil and criminal cases, requiring authentication and verification to establish the authenticity, authorship, and reliability of digital artifacts presented as evidence. Command-line tools such as 'exiftool' or 'ffprobe' enable examiners to extract metadata, analyze file attributes, and validate digital signatures, verifying the integrity and provenance of digital evidence in forensic investigations and courtroom proceedings.

Moreover, laws governing digital evidence encompass rules of procedure and evidentiary standards that govern the admissibility of electronic records, forensic reports, and expert testimony in legal proceedings. Forensic examiners use commands like 'openssl' or 'hashdeep' to calculate hash values, create digital certificates, and generate forensic reports documenting findings, ensuring accuracy, completeness, and reliability of expert testimony presented to judges and juries in criminal trials or civil litigation cases.

In addition to procedural rules, laws governing digital evidence address privacy concerns, data protection regulations, and constitutional rights that safeguard individuals' privacy rights, limiting the scope of digital evidence collection, retention, and disclosure in compliance with Fourth Amendment protections against unreasonable searches and seizures. By conducting forensic examinations in accordance with legal mandates and obtaining court-authorized warrants, forensic examiners can use commands like 'dd' or 'ddrescue' to create forensic disk images, preserving original evidence and ensuring compliance with legal requirements governing data acquisition, preservation, and analysis in digital forensics.

Furthermore, laws governing digital evidence address the admissibility of forensic tools and methodologies used in data recovery, analysis, and preservation, requiring validation, reliability testing, and expert testimony to demonstrate the scientific reliability and probative value of digital evidence presented in court. Command-line tools such as 'autopsy' or 'sleuthkit' enable examiners to conduct file system analysis, keyword searches, and timeline reconstruction, facilitating the identification and preservation of digital evidence relevant to criminal investigations or civil litigation matters.

Additionally, laws governing digital evidence include rules of evidence that regulate the use of electronic surveillance, digital forensics, and cybersecurity measures in law enforcement investigations, ensuring compliance with legal standards, privacy protections, and due process rights guaranteed under the Constitution. By adhering to legal requirements and obtaining court-issued subpoenas or search warrants, forensic examiners can use commands like 'netstat' or 'tcpdump' to capture network traffic, monitor communication channels, and identify unauthorized access attempts or cyber threats, supporting criminal investigations and safeguarding digital evidence against suppression or exclusion in court.

Moreover, laws governing digital evidence encompass jurisdictional considerations, international treaties, and mutual legal assistance agreements that govern the exchange, sharing, and transfer of digital evidence between countries, ensuring cooperation, coordination, and mutual respect for legal systems and procedural rules governing cross-border investigations. Command-line tools such as 'rsync' or 'scp' enable examiners to securely transfer encrypted files, digital artifacts, and forensic reports between jurisdictions, complying with legal mandates and preserving chain of custody in international cybercrime investigations or transnational legal proceedings.

In summary, laws governing digital evidence establish a comprehensive legal framework that regulates the collection, admissibility, and use of digital artifacts in legal proceedings, ensuring fairness, reliability, and integrity in the judicial process. By adhering to procedural rules, evidentiary standards, and privacy protections, forensic examiners can use command-line tools and forensic techniques to collect, analyze, and authenticate digital evidence, supporting criminal investigations, civil litigation, and regulatory enforcement actions while respecting constitutional rights and legal principles governing digital evidence admissibility. Ethical guidelines for forensic analysts are essential principles and standards that govern professional conduct, integrity, and responsibility in the practice of digital forensics, ensuring adherence to ethical norms, legal requirements, and industry best practices. These guidelines encompass ethical considerations such as confidentiality, impartiality, transparency, and respect for privacy rights, guiding forensic analysts in their interactions with clients, colleagues, stakeholders, and the broader community. Command-line tools such as 'grep' or 'awk' enable analysts to search and analyze ethical codes of conduct, regulatory standards, and professional guidelines, facilitating compliance with ethical principles and ethical decision-making in digital forensic investigations.

Confidentiality is a fundamental ethical principle in digital forensics, requiring analysts to protect sensitive information, client data, and investigative findings from unauthorized access, disclosure, or misuse. By using commands like 'chmod' or 'chown' to set file permissions and access controls, forensic analysts can restrict access to confidential case files, forensic reports, and evidence repositories, ensuring confidentiality and data protection in compliance with ethical standards and legal obligations governing client confidentiality and privileged communications.

Impartiality and objectivity are critical ethical principles that require forensic analysts to conduct investigations with fairness, neutrality, and independence, avoiding bias, conflicts of interest, or undue influence that may compromise the integrity or impartiality of forensic findings. Command-line tools such as 'md5deep' or 'sha256sum' enable analysts to calculate hash values, verify data integrity, and detect unauthorized alterations or tampering in forensic evidence, ensuring objectivity and reliability in forensic examinations conducted in accordance with ethical guidelines and professional standards.

Transparency is an ethical principle that emphasizes openness, honesty, and accountability in forensic investigations, requiring analysts to disclose methodologies, techniques, and limitations associated with digital forensic tools and procedures used to collect, analyze, and interpret digital evidence. By using commands like 'autopsy' or 'sleuthkit' to conduct file system analysis and keyword searches, forensic analysts can document forensic processes, document findings, and provide detailed explanations of forensic methodologies and techniques employed in forensic examinations, ensuring transparency and clarity in communication with stakeholders, legal counsel, and judicial authorities.

Respect for privacy rights is a fundamental ethical principle that requires forensic analysts to safeguard individuals' privacy, confidentiality, and data protection rights when collecting, analyzing, and disclosing digital evidence in forensic investigations. By conducting forensic examinations in accordance with legal mandates and obtaining court-issued subpoenas or search warrants, forensic analysts can use commands like 'dd' or 'ddrescue' to create forensic disk images, preserve original evidence, and ensure compliance with legal requirements governing data acquisition, preservation, and analysis in digital forensics.

Professional competence and continuous professional development are ethical principles that require forensic analysts to maintain proficiency, expertise, and knowledge in emerging technologies, forensic methodologies, and legal developments relevant to digital forensics. By using commands like 'man' or 'info' to access documentation, manuals, and guides on forensic procedures, best practices, and industry standards, forensic analysts can enhance competence and ethical decision-making in digital forensic investigations, supporting professional growth and adherence to ethical guidelines governing forensic practice.

Integrity and honesty are ethical principles that require forensic analysts to maintain honesty, integrity, and trustworthiness in their interactions with clients, colleagues, stakeholders, and the public, avoiding misrepresentation, deception, or unethical behavior that may undermine the credibility or reputation of forensic science and digital forensics. By using commands like 'openssl' or 'hashdeep' to calculate hash values, create digital certificates, and generate forensic reports documenting findings, forensic analysts can demonstrate integrity and reliability in forensic examinations conducted in accordance with ethical standards and professional ethics codes.

Furthermore, ethical guidelines for forensic analysts encompass accountability and responsibility for their actions, decisions, and professional conduct in digital forensic investigations, requiring analysts to adhere to ethical principles, legal requirements, and industry best practices to ensure fairness, transparency, and integrity in the administration of justice. Command-line tools such as 'grep' or 'awk' facilitate search and analysis of ethical codes of conduct, regulatory standards, and professional guidelines, enabling analysts to promote ethical behavior, accountability, and responsibility in digital forensic practice.

In summary, ethical guidelines for forensic analysts provide essential principles and standards that govern professional conduct, integrity, and responsibility in the practice of digital forensics, ensuring adherence to ethical norms, legal requirements, and industry best practices. By following ethical principles such as confidentiality, impartiality, transparency, respect for privacy rights, professional competence, integrity, and accountability, forensic analysts can conduct ethical, fair, and reliable digital forensic investigations that uphold the highest standards of professionalism and contribute to the administration of justice

## Chapter 8: Data Recovery Techniques for iOS Devices

Understanding data recovery methods is crucial in digital forensics, encompassing techniques and procedures used to retrieve, reconstruct, and restore digital information from storage media, devices, and systems that have experienced data loss, corruption, or deletion. Forensic analysts deploy specialized tools and methodologies to recover deleted files, extract hidden data, and reconstruct damaged or fragmented files from hard drives, solid-state drives (SSDs), memory cards, and other storage devices using commands such as 'ddrescue' or 'testdisk' to create disk images and perform file system repairs, ensuring data integrity and preserving evidentiary value in forensic investigations.

Data recovery methods involve both logical and physical techniques tailored to recover different types of data and address various causes of data loss or corruption. Logical data recovery focuses on retrieving deleted files, folders, and application data from intact file systems and storage media, utilizing commands like 'photorec' or 'scalpel' to perform file carving and data extraction from fragmented or damaged storage devices, reconstructing file structures and recovering digital artifacts such as documents, photos, and multimedia files in forensic examinations.

Physical data recovery techniques are employed to retrieve data from physically damaged or inaccessible storage media, including hard drives with mechanical failures, SSDs with NAND flash chip issues, and memory cards affected by physical damage or electronic faults. Forensic analysts use commands like 'dd' or 'ddrescue' to create forensic disk images and perform bit-by-bit data cloning, bypassing damaged sectors or bad blocks to preserve data integrity and facilitate data reconstruction from defective storage devices in digital forensic investigations.

Moreover, data recovery methods include forensic data acquisition techniques used to collect and preserve digital evidence from computers, mobile devices, and network servers in forensic investigations. By using commands like 'dd' or 'dcfldd' to create forensic disk images, forensic analysts capture exact copies of storage media, ensuring data integrity and chain of custody compliance while preserving original evidence for forensic analysis and examination using specialized forensic tools and methodologies.

Forensic data recovery also encompasses live forensics techniques employed to acquire volatile data and system artifacts from running operating systems and active processes, facilitating real-time analysis and preservation of digital evidence in forensic investigations. Commands such as 'ps' or 'netstat' enable analysts to list active processes, monitor network connections, and capture volatile data such as running applications, open files, and network activities, providing insights into user activities, system configurations, and potential security incidents affecting computer systems and network environments.

Additionally, data recovery methods include mobile device forensics techniques used to retrieve, analyze, and extract digital evidence from smartphones, tablets, and wearable devices running iOS, Android, or other mobile operating systems. Forensic analysts use commands like 'adb' (Android Debug Bridge) or 'ideviceinfo' to access device information, retrieve device logs, and perform data acquisition from mobile devices, recovering call logs, SMS messages, photos, and application data for forensic examination and analysis using specialized forensic software and tools.

Furthermore, data recovery methods encompass network forensics techniques used to capture, analyze, and reconstruct digital evidence from network communications, including packet captures, log files, and network traffic data. Commands like 'tcpdump' or 'Wireshark' enable analysts to capture network packets, filter traffic based on protocol or IP address, and analyze communication patterns to identify malicious activities, unauthorized access attempts, or data exfiltration incidents occurring over network channels, supporting forensic investigations and incident response efforts in cybersecurity operations.

Moreover, data recovery methods include database forensics techniques used to recover, analyze, and extract digital evidence from relational databases,

NoSQL databases, and cloud-based data storage solutions. Forensic analysts use commands like 'sqlmap' or 'nosqlmap' to perform SQL injection tests and database penetration testing, identifying vulnerabilities, and retrieving sensitive data stored in database systems for forensic examination, analysis, and incident response in data breach investigations and cybersecurity incidents.

Additionally, data recovery methods encompass file system analysis techniques used to examine file structures, metadata attributes, and file content stored on storage media and file systems. Commands like 'fsstat' or 'fls' enable analysts to retrieve file system statistics, list allocated and deleted files, and analyze directory structures to reconstruct file paths, recover deleted files, and identify digital artifacts relevant to forensic investigations, ensuring data integrity and evidentiary value in legal proceedings.

Furthermore, data recovery methods include forensic data carving techniques used to extract, reconstruct, and recover digital artifacts from unallocated space, fragmented files, and damaged storage media. Forensic analysts use commands like 'scalpel' or 'foremost' to perform file carving and data extraction from raw disk images, identifying file signatures, and reconstructing digital artifacts such as documents, images, videos, and email attachments for forensic analysis and evidentiary presentation in criminal investigations and civil litigation cases.

In summary, understanding data recovery methods in digital forensics involves deploying specialized techniques and tools to retrieve, reconstruct, and restore digital information from storage media, devices, and systems affected by data loss, corruption, or deletion. By employing logical and physical data recovery techniques, forensic analysts can recover deleted files, reconstruct damaged data, and preserve evidentiary value in forensic investigations using command-line tools and forensic methodologies tailored to address various causes of data loss and support legal proceedings. Overcoming encryption challenges in digital forensics involves navigating the complexities of encrypted data to access, recover, and analyze information crucial to investigations, despite cryptographic protections designed to secure sensitive data from unauthorized access or tampering. Encryption poses significant challenges to forensic analysts seeking to retrieve data from devices, files, or communications that employ strong encryption algorithms and secure cryptographic keys. Command-line tools such as 'openssl' or 'gnupg' facilitate encryption and decryption operations, enabling forensic analysts to decrypt files, recover plaintext data, and bypass encryption barriers in forensic examinations using established cryptographic techniques and methodologies.

Encryption challenges in digital forensics extend to encrypted storage media, such as hard drives, solid-state drives (SSDs), and USB devices, where data is protected using full-disk encryption (FDE) or file-based encryption mechanisms that prevent unauthorized access to stored information. Forensic analysts use commands like 'dm-crypt' or 'BitLocker' to manage encrypted volumes, recover encryption keys, and perform disk imaging techniques to create forensic copies of encrypted storage media, ensuring data integrity and preserving evidentiary value in forensic investigations involving encrypted storage devices.

Moreover, encryption challenges include encrypted file containers and archives, such as encrypted ZIP files, VeraCrypt volumes, and encrypted email attachments, which require forensic analysts to use commands like '7z' or 'veracrypt' to mount encrypted volumes, retrieve decryption keys, and extract plaintext data for forensic analysis, overcoming encryption barriers and accessing digital evidence stored in encrypted formats.

Encryption challenges in digital forensics also encompass encrypted communications, such as encrypted emails, instant messages, and VoIP calls, where data is protected using end-to-end encryption (E2EE) or secure communication protocols that prevent interception or monitoring of transmitted information. Forensic analysts use commands like 'wireshark' or 'tshark' to capture network packets, decrypt encrypted traffic, and reconstruct communication sessions to retrieve plaintext messages, attachments, and metadata for forensic examination and analysis, overcoming encryption challenges in network forensics investigations.

Furthermore, encryption challenges include mobile device encryption, where smartphones, tablets, and wearable devices use encryption mechanisms to protect user data stored on device storage or external memory cards. Forensic analysts use commands like 'adb' (Android Debug Bridge) or 'ideviceinfo' to access device information, bypass device locks, and perform data acquisition from encrypted mobile devices, recovering encrypted app data, photos, and messages for forensic analysis and evidentiary presentation in criminal investigations and legal proceedings.

Additionally, encryption challenges encompass cloud-based encryption, where data stored in cloud services and platforms is protected using encryption techniques and secure access controls to prevent unauthorized access or data breaches. Forensic analysts use commands like 'rclone' or 'aws s3' to interact with cloud storage APIs, retrieve encrypted data, and decrypt files stored in cloud repositories, overcoming encryption challenges in cloud forensics investigations and preserving evidentiary value in digital evidence collected from cloud-based environments.

Moreover, encryption challenges include memory encryption, where volatile data stored in computer RAM (Random Access Memory) is protected using memory encryption mechanisms that prevent unauthorized access or extraction of sensitive information during live forensics investigations. Forensic analysts use commands like 'volatility' or 'winpmem' to capture memory dumps, analyze memory structures, and recover plaintext data from encrypted memory segments, overcoming encryption challenges in volatile data acquisition and preserving digital evidence for forensic analysis and incident response in cybersecurity investigations.

Furthermore, encryption challenges encompass encryption key management and recovery, where cryptographic keys used to encrypt and decrypt data are crucial for accessing encrypted information in forensic examinations. Forensic analysts use commands like 'keytool' or 'openssl' to manage encryption keys, recover lost or deleted keys, and decrypt encrypted data stored on devices or in encrypted containers, overcoming encryption challenges and accessing plaintext data essential for investigative purposes in digital forensics and cybersecurity operations.

In summary, overcoming encryption challenges in digital forensics requires forensic analysts to employ specialized tools, techniques, and command-line methodologies to decrypt encrypted data, recover encryption keys, and bypass encryption barriers to access, retrieve, and analyze digital evidence crucial to investigations. By navigating encryption complexities and adhering to legal and ethical guidelines governing data privacy and security, forensic analysts can overcome encryption challenges, preserve evidentiary value, and support the administration of justice in criminal investigations, civil litigation, and regulatory compliance matters

## Chapter 9: Introduction to iOS App Analysis

App sandboxing and security measures are critical components of modern operating systems and software applications, designed to mitigate security risks, protect user data, and prevent unauthorized access or malicious activities within confined application environments. Sandboxing restricts the privileges and resources available to applications, limiting their interaction with system resources and other applications to enhance security and mitigate potential vulnerabilities. Commands like 'sandbox-exec' or 'firejail' enable administrators to create sandbox profiles, define access controls, and enforce security policies for individual applications or processes, ensuring isolation and containment of potential threats in sandboxed environments deployed in digital forensics and cybersecurity operations.

App sandboxing is implemented using techniques such as process isolation, where applications run in isolated environments with restricted access to system resources, files, and network connections to prevent malicious activities or unauthorized data access. Command-line tools like 'docker' or 'podman' facilitate containerization, enabling administrators to create lightweight, isolated containers for running applications, services, or forensic tools in secure, sandboxed environments without compromising system integrity or exposing sensitive data to potential threats in digital forensics investigations.

Furthermore, app sandboxing includes privilege separation, where applications are separated into distinct processes with limited privileges and permissions to reduce the impact of security breaches or compromised software components. Commands like 'sudo' or 'runuser' enable administrators to execute commands with elevated privileges or switch to different user contexts, implementing privilege separation techniques to minimize the risk of unauthorized access or privilege escalation in sandboxed environments used for forensic analysis or cybersecurity operations.

Moreover, app sandboxing incorporates file system restrictions, where applications are confined to designated directories or file paths with restricted read, write, or execute permissions to prevent unauthorized file access or modification. Command-line utilities such as 'chroot' or 'mount' enable administrators to create chroot environments or mount file systems with restricted access controls, ensuring data integrity and preventing malware or malicious code from accessing sensitive files or system resources in sandboxed environments deployed for digital forensics examinations or incident response activities.

Additionally, app sandboxing includes network isolation, where applications are isolated from external networks or restricted to specific network segments with controlled access to prevent unauthorized communication, data exfiltration, or network-based attacks. Commands like 'iptables' or 'firewalld' facilitate firewall configuration and network packet filtering, implementing network segmentation and access controls to limit outbound and inbound network traffic in sandboxed environments used for forensic investigations or cybersecurity operations.

Furthermore, app sandboxing incorporates memory protection mechanisms, where applications are safeguarded against memory-based attacks, buffer overflows, or memory corruption vulnerabilities that could compromise system integrity or expose sensitive data to unauthorized access. Command-line tools such as 'grsecurity' or 'AddressSanitizer' enable administrators to deploy memory protection techniques, including address space layout randomization (ASLR) or memory leak detection, to detect and mitigate memory-related vulnerabilities in sandboxed environments used for digital forensics analysis or software development.

Moreover, app sandboxing includes runtime integrity checks, where applications undergo continuous monitoring, auditing, or runtime verification to detect and respond to suspicious activities, unauthorized modifications, or security incidents in real-time. Commands like 'auditd' or 'sysdig' enable administrators to monitor system calls, file access patterns, and process activities, implementing runtime integrity checks and security auditing in sandboxed environments to detect anomalies, log events, and investigate potential security breaches in digital forensics investigations or cybersecurity incident response.

Additionally, app sandboxing incorporates cryptographic protections, where sensitive data stored or transmitted by applications is encrypted using strong encryption algorithms and secure cryptographic keys to protect against data breaches, unauthorized access, or data tampering. Command-line utilities such as 'openssl' or 'gpg' facilitate encryption and decryption operations, enabling administrators to implement cryptographic protections for sensitive data stored in sandboxed environments or transmitted over insecure networks, ensuring data confidentiality, integrity, and authenticity in digital forensics examinations and cybersecurity operations.

Furthermore, app sandboxing includes auditing and logging mechanisms, where applications generate audit trails, log files, or security events to record user activities, system events, or access attempts for forensic analysis, incident response, or compliance auditing purposes. Commands like 'auditctl' or 'syslog-ng' enable administrators to configure auditing policies, monitor log files, and collect forensic evidence in sandboxed environments to investigate security incidents, trace malicious activities, and support legal proceedings or regulatory compliance requirements in digital forensics and cybersecurity operations.

In summary, app sandboxing and security measures are essential strategies for mitigating security risks, protecting user data, and preventing unauthorized access or malicious activities in digital forensics and cybersecurity operations. By implementing sandboxing techniques, process isolation, privilege separation, file system restrictions, network isolation, memory protection, runtime integrity checks, cryptographic protections, auditing, and logging mechanisms using command-line tools and techniques, administrators can enhance system security, ensure data integrity, and preserve evidentiary value in forensic investigations and incident response activities. Extracting data from third-party apps is a crucial aspect of digital forensics, involving techniques and methodologies to access and retrieve information stored within applications not native to the operating system or standard software suite. Forensic analysts utilize specialized tools and command-line utilities such as 'adb' (Android Debug Bridge) or 'ideviceinfo' to interface with mobile devices, retrieve application data, and extract information from third-party apps installed on smartphones or tablets running Android or iOS operating systems, facilitating forensic examinations and investigative analysis of messaging apps, social media platforms, and productivity tools used for communication and data storage in digital forensic investigations.

One common approach to extracting data from third-party apps involves acquiring forensic images of mobile devices, creating exact copies of device storage that include app data stored in encrypted or unencrypted formats. Commands like 'dd' (data duplicator) or 'dcfldd' are used to create forensic images of Android devices, capturing complete snapshots of device storage including installed apps and their associated data files, ensuring data integrity and preserving evidentiary value in forensic investigations where extracting third-party app data is essential for reconstructing user activities, communications, or digital evidence relevant to criminal or civil cases.

Moreover, extracting data from third-party apps requires forensic analysts to bypass device locks or encryption protections to access application data stored in secure containers or encrypted databases. Commands like 'adb backup' or 'iTunes backup' enable analysts to create device backups, extract encrypted backups using decryption keys or password recovery tools, and recover plaintext data from third-party apps such as messaging apps, social networking platforms, or cloud storage services used for storing personal or business-related information, facilitating comprehensive forensic analysis and investigative reporting in digital forensic examinations.

Additionally, extracting data from third-party apps involves employing forensic data acquisition techniques to retrieve app-specific data stored in SQLite databases, cache files, or application directories on mobile devices. Command-line tools such as 'sqlite3' or 'adb shell' enable analysts to query SQLite databases, extract tables, view records, and analyze structured data stored by third-party apps, recovering user interactions, chat histories, media files, or location data relevant to forensic investigations involving mobile device usage and digital evidence recovery from popular apps used for communication, social networking, or online transactions.

Furthermore, extracting data from third-party apps includes utilizing file carving techniques to recover deleted files, attachments, or media shared within apps that store data in unallocated space or fragmented storage areas on mobile devices. Command-line utilities like 'photorec' or 'foremost' enable analysts to perform file carving operations, scan device storage for file headers and footers associated with specific file types, and reconstruct deleted or lost data fragments from third-party apps, facilitating forensic data recovery and evidence preservation in investigations involving digital evidence recovery from mobile devices and applications.

Moreover, extracting data from third-party apps involves analyzing application metadata, configuration files, and user preferences stored on devices or cloud-based storage platforms accessed using command-line interfaces such as 'rclone' or 's3cmd', enabling analysts to retrieve app-related information, analyze user settings, and reconstruct application usage patterns for forensic examination and investigative reporting in cases where digital evidence from third-party apps is critical to establishing timelines, user intent, or communication patterns relevant to criminal investigations or civil litigation involving mobile device usage and data privacy issues.

In summary, extracting data from third-party apps in digital forensics requires forensic analysts to deploy specialized tools, command-line utilities, and forensic techniques to access, retrieve, and analyze application-specific data stored on mobile devices, ensuring data integrity, preserving evidentiary value, and supporting investigative efforts in criminal or civil cases where extracting third-party app data is essential for reconstructing digital evidence, establishing facts, and presenting findings in legal proceedings or regulatory compliance matters concerning mobile device usage and data privacy concerns

## Chapter 10: Case Studies in iOS Digital Investigations

Forensic analysis of social media apps is a critical aspect of digital investigations, focusing on extracting, analyzing, and interpreting digital evidence from popular social networking platforms used for communication, sharing content, and interacting with others online. Analysts employ specialized tools and command-line utilities such as 'ExifTool' or 'foremost' to examine metadata embedded in photos or files shared on social media platforms, enabling detailed forensic analysis of timestamps, geolocation data, and user interactions to reconstruct timelines and activities relevant to digital forensic examinations involving social media usage.

One fundamental approach to forensic analysis of social media apps involves capturing forensic images of devices used to access social media platforms, preserving data integrity and ensuring the admissibility of digital evidence in legal proceedings. Commands like 'dd' (data duplicator) or 'dcfldd' facilitate the creation of forensic images of mobile devices or computers, capturing device storage including installed social media apps, user profiles, chat histories, and multimedia content shared or accessed through social networking platforms, facilitating comprehensive forensic analysis and evidentiary preservation in investigations involving digital evidence derived from social media usage.

Moreover, forensic analysis of social media apps requires analysts to extract and examine user-generated content, such as text posts, comments, and private messages exchanged within social networking platforms. Command-line tools like 'sqlite3' or 'adb shell' enable analysts to query SQLite databases stored on devices or cloud servers, extract message threads, analyze communication patterns, and reconstruct conversations relevant to forensic investigations involving social media platforms used for personal communications, online interactions, or business-related activities.

Additionally, forensic analysis of social media apps involves utilizing digital forensic techniques to recover deleted or hidden content shared on social networking platforms, including photos, videos, or multimedia files stored in temporary cache or unallocated storage space on mobile devices. Command-line utilities like 'photorec' or 'scalpel' enable analysts to perform file carving operations, scan device storage for fragmented or deleted data fragments associated with social media apps, and reconstruct deleted content for forensic examination and evidentiary presentation in digital forensic investigations involving social media evidence recovery and data reconstruction.

Furthermore, forensic analysis of social media apps includes analyzing user profiles, metadata, and digital footprints left behind by individuals using social networking platforms to interact, share information, or engage in online activities. Command-line interfaces such as 'grep' or 'awk' facilitate pattern matching, data extraction, and keyword searching within log files, configuration files, or cached data associated with social media apps installed on devices, enabling analysts to identify user accounts, track user activities, and establish digital evidence linking individuals to specific actions or events in forensic investigations involving social media usage and online behavior.

Moreover, forensic analysis of social media apps encompasses examining privacy settings, account permissions, and data access controls implemented by social networking platforms to protect user information and regulate access to personal data shared online. Command-line utilities like 'curl' or 'requests' enable analysts to interact with social media APIs, retrieve user profile information, and analyze data permissions, ensuring compliance with legal requirements and ethical guidelines governing the collection, handling, and analysis of digital evidence derived from social media platforms in forensic investigations or litigation proceedings involving privacy rights and data protection issues.

Additionally, forensic analysis of social media apps involves interpreting digital evidence within the context of social networking platforms used for digital marketing, online advertising, or brand promotion, leveraging command-line tools like 'grep' or 'jq' to extract metadata, analyze user engagement metrics, and assess the impact of social media activities on consumer behavior or corporate reputation in forensic investigations involving social media analytics and digital marketing strategies employed by businesses or individuals using social networking platforms for commercial purposes.

In summary, forensic analysis of social media apps requires forensic analysts to deploy specialized tools, command-line utilities, and digital forensic techniques to extract, analyze, and interpret digital evidence derived from social networking platforms used for communication, content sharing, and online interactions. By employing forensic imaging, data extraction, file carving, metadata analysis, and API interaction using command-line interfaces, analysts can uncover relevant digital evidence, reconstruct user activities, and present findings in legal proceedings or investigative reports concerning social media usage, digital communications, or online behavior patterns relevant to digital forensic examinations and cybersecurity investigations. Incident response in iOS data breaches involves a structured approach to detecting, containing, and mitigating security incidents that compromise the confidentiality, integrity, or availability of data stored on iOS devices, emphasizing rapid identification and response to security breaches to minimize impact and restore normal operations. Forensic analysts and incident response teams utilize specialized tools and command-line utilities such as 'ideviceinfo' or 'ssh' to access iOS devices remotely, collect volatile data, and analyze system logs to identify indicators of compromise (IOCs), facilitating swift incident response actions and forensic investigations in iOS data breach scenarios.

One essential aspect of incident response in iOS data breaches is establishing incident detection mechanisms to monitor device activity, network traffic, and application behavior for signs of unauthorized access, malware infections, or suspicious activities indicative of a security breach. Commands like 'tcpdump' or 'syslog-ng' enable analysts to capture network packets, monitor communication channels, and log system events in real-time, facilitating proactive incident detection and timely response to security incidents affecting iOS devices and associated digital assets.

Moreover, incident response in iOS data breaches involves conducting forensic data acquisition to preserve volatile data and collect forensic evidence from compromised devices using command-line tools such as 'dd' (data duplicator) or 'iTunes backup', enabling analysts to create forensic images, extract encrypted backups, and recover digital evidence stored on iOS devices for forensic analysis and evidentiary preservation in data breach investigations involving unauthorized access, data theft, or cyber-attacks targeting sensitive information stored on mobile devices.

Additionally, incident response in iOS data breaches includes conducting malware analysis and forensic examination of malicious software or unauthorized applications installed on compromised devices using command-line utilities like 'sandbox-exec' or 'frida', enabling analysts to analyze app behavior, detect malicious code, and identify attack vectors used to exploit vulnerabilities or compromise iOS security mechanisms, facilitating incident containment and remediation efforts to mitigate the impact of malware infections or unauthorized access in iOS data breach incidents.

Furthermore, incident response in iOS data breaches involves performing memory forensics and volatile data analysis using command-line tools such as 'volatility' or 'winpmem', enabling analysts to capture memory dumps, analyze process memory, and identify running processes or malicious activities in memory-intensive applications to detect, contain, and investigate security incidents affecting iOS devices and sensitive data stored in volatile memory locations.

Moreover, incident response in iOS data breaches encompasses conducting forensic analysis of file systems and storage media using command-line utilities like 'fsck' or 'mount', enabling analysts to repair file system errors, recover deleted files, and perform data carving operations to reconstruct fragmented data structures or restore deleted information from compromised iOS devices, facilitating data recovery and evidentiary preservation in forensic investigations involving data breaches or unauthorized access incidents affecting iOS platforms.

Moreover, incident response in iOS data breaches involves analyzing network traffic and connections using command-line tools such as 'tshark' or 'tcpdump', enabling analysts to capture and analyze network packets, monitor communication channels, and identify anomalous activities or suspicious traffic patterns indicative of unauthorized access, data exfiltration, or network-based attacks targeting iOS devices and sensitive data stored on mobile platforms.

Additionally, incident response in iOS data breaches includes conducting forensic timeline analysis and digital evidence reconstruction using command-line utilities like 'grep' or 'awk', enabling analysts to search log files, analyze system events, and reconstruct user activities or data access patterns to establish timelines, identify attack vectors, and attribute security incidents to specific events or actions in forensic investigations involving iOS data breaches and digital forensic examinations of compromised mobile devices.

Furthermore, incident response in iOS data breaches encompasses coordinating with legal and compliance teams to ensure regulatory compliance and facilitate legal proceedings involving data breach notifications, incident reporting, and evidence presentation in litigation or regulatory investigations concerning iOS security breaches and data privacy violations affecting sensitive information stored on mobile devices.

In summary, incident response in iOS data breaches requires forensic analysts and incident response teams to deploy specialized tools, command-line utilities, and digital forensic techniques to detect, contain, and mitigate security incidents affecting iOS devices, ensuring timely incident response, effective data breach remediation, and evidentiary preservation in forensic investigations involving unauthorized access, malware infections, or cyber-attacks targeting sensitive information stored on iOS platforms

**BOOK 2**
**IOS FORENSICS 101**
**TECHNIQUES FOR EXTRACTING LOGICAL DATA**

**ROB BOTWRIGHT**

# Chapter 1: Overview of Logical Data Extraction

Understanding the logical extraction process in digital forensics involves a methodical approach to accessing and retrieving data from electronic devices, focusing on acquiring user-generated content, application data, and system files stored on devices without altering the original data or compromising evidentiary integrity. Forensic analysts utilize specialized tools and techniques, including command-line utilities such as 'adb' (Android Debug Bridge) or 'idevicebackup2' to initiate logical extraction processes on Android or iOS devices, facilitating data acquisition and forensic analysis in investigations involving digital evidence recovery, data preservation, and evidentiary presentation in legal proceedings or regulatory investigations.

Logical extraction begins with establishing a forensic acquisition plan, identifying target devices, and selecting appropriate tools and command-line utilities to initiate the data extraction process while adhering to legal and procedural guidelines governing digital evidence handling and chain of custody requirements in digital forensics examinations and investigative activities. Commands like 'adb shell' or 'ideviceinfo' enable analysts to access device information, retrieve system logs, and gather device metadata to facilitate initial assessment and planning for logical data extraction processes in digital forensic investigations.

Moreover, understanding the logical extraction process involves creating forensic backups or images of devices using command-line tools such as 'dd' (data duplicator) or 'itool' (iTunes command-line utility) to capture device storage, including installed applications, user data, and system configurations, ensuring data integrity and preserving evidentiary value for forensic analysis and investigative reporting in cases involving criminal activities, civil disputes, or regulatory compliance issues affecting digital evidence and electronic data stored on mobile devices.

Additionally, logical extraction encompasses retrieving user-generated content, application data, and multimedia files stored in accessible directories or system partitions on mobile devices using command-line utilities such as 'adb pull' or 'idevicebackup2', enabling analysts to extract text messages, call logs, photos, videos, and application-specific data from Android or iOS devices for forensic examination and evidentiary presentation in digital forensics investigations involving mobile device usage and data recovery from electronic devices.

Furthermore, understanding the logical extraction process involves analyzing application data stored in SQLite databases, cache files, or application directories using command-line tools like 'sqlite3' or 'adb shell', enabling analysts to query database tables, extract records, and analyze structured data associated with installed applications or system services on Android or iOS devices, facilitating forensic analysis of communication patterns, user interactions, and digital evidence relevant to criminal investigations or civil litigation involving electronic data stored on mobile platforms.

Moreover, logical extraction includes retrieving metadata and system logs from mobile devices using command-line utilities such as 'syslog-ng' or 'logcat', enabling analysts to monitor system events, capture log entries, and document device activities in real-time for forensic analysis and incident response in cases involving security incidents, data breaches, or unauthorized access to electronic devices and sensitive information stored on mobile platforms.

Additionally, understanding the logical extraction process encompasses capturing network traffic and communication logs using command-line tools such as 'tcpdump' or 'wireshark', enabling analysts to intercept and analyze network packets, monitor data transmissions, and investigate network-based attacks or suspicious activities affecting Android or iOS devices, facilitating forensic analysis of digital evidence related to online communications, data transfers, or remote access incidents involving mobile device usage and network security monitoring in digital forensics investigations.

Furthermore, logical extraction involves documenting forensic findings, preparing detailed reports, and presenting forensic evidence in a clear, concise manner using command-line tools such as 'grep' or 'awk', enabling analysts to search log files, filter data, and extract relevant information for investigative analysis, evidentiary presentation, or expert testimony in legal proceedings involving digital evidence recovery, data breach investigations, or regulatory compliance matters affecting electronic data stored on mobile devices.

In summary, understanding the logical extraction process in digital forensics requires forensic analysts to deploy specialized tools, command-line utilities, and investigative techniques to access, retrieve, and analyze electronic data stored on Android or iOS devices, ensuring comprehensive data acquisition, evidentiary preservation, and forensic analysis in investigations involving mobile device usage, digital evidence recovery, and legal proceedings requiring expert testimony or evidentiary presentation concerning electronic data and digital forensics examinations. Logical extraction in digital forensics offers significant benefits and presents certain limitations, shaping its role in acquiring and analyzing data from electronic devices without altering the original content or compromising forensic integrity. Forensic analysts utilize command-line tools and specialized software like 'adb' (Android Debug Bridge) or 'idevicebackup2' to initiate logical extraction processes on Android or iOS devices, enabling the retrieval of user-generated content, application data, and system files essential for forensic analysis and evidentiary presentation in legal proceedings, regulatory investigations, or cybersecurity incidents involving digital evidence and electronic data stored on mobile platforms.

The primary benefit of logical extraction lies in its non-invasive nature, allowing forensic analysts to retrieve data from devices without modifying or altering the original content, ensuring data integrity and preserving evidentiary value for forensic analysis and investigative reporting. Commands such as 'adb pull' or 'idevicebackup2' enable analysts to extract text messages, call logs, photos, videos, and application-specific data from Android or iOS devices, facilitating comprehensive data acquisition and forensic examination of digital evidence relevant to criminal investigations, civil litigation, or regulatory compliance issues involving mobile device usage and electronic data recovery.

Moreover, logical extraction offers scalability and efficiency in acquiring data from multiple devices simultaneously using command-line utilities like 'adb shell' or 'itool', enabling analysts to deploy batch processing techniques and automate data extraction workflows to streamline forensic investigations and expedite the retrieval of digital evidence from Android or iOS devices in cases involving large-scale data breaches, corporate investigations, or law enforcement operations requiring swift response and effective management of digital evidence recovery tasks.

Additionally, logical extraction facilitates targeted data acquisition from specific applications, directories, or system partitions on mobile devices using command-line tools such as 'sqlite3' or 'adb pull', enabling analysts to query SQLite databases, extract records, and analyze structured data associated with installed applications or user activities on Android or iOS platforms, supporting forensic analysis of communication patterns, social media interactions, and digital evidence relevant to criminal prosecutions or civil disputes involving electronic data stored on mobile devices.

Furthermore, logical extraction enables forensic analysts to retrieve metadata and system logs from Android or iOS devices using command-line utilities like 'syslog-ng' or 'logcat', enabling real-time monitoring of system events, capturing log entries, and documenting device activities for forensic analysis and incident response in cases involving security incidents, data breaches, or unauthorized access to electronic devices and sensitive information stored on mobile platforms, enhancing forensic capabilities and ensuring compliance with legal and procedural guidelines governing digital evidence handling and chain of custody requirements in digital forensics examinations.

However, logical extraction has certain limitations, including its dependency on device accessibility and administrative privileges required to initiate data extraction processes using command-line interfaces such as 'sudo' or 'root', limiting the scope of forensic analysis and data recovery efforts in cases where devices are locked, encrypted, or protected by security measures designed to prevent unauthorized access or tampering with electronic data stored on mobile platforms, posing challenges to forensic investigations and data recovery operations requiring advanced techniques and specialized tools to overcome encryption barriers or device lockdown mechanisms.

Moreover, logical extraction may encounter obstacles related to data fragmentation, file system errors, or data corruption affecting the reliability and completeness of extracted data sets retrieved from Android or iOS devices using command-line utilities such as 'fsck' or 'mount', necessitating forensic analysts to employ data validation techniques and error-checking procedures to verify data integrity, identify data anomalies, and address technical challenges impacting the accuracy and reliability of forensic findings presented as digital evidence in legal proceedings or regulatory investigations involving electronic data stored on mobile devices.

Additionally, logical extraction may involve time-consuming processes and resource-intensive tasks requiring forensic analysts to allocate sufficient time and manpower resources to execute data extraction workflows using command-line tools such as 'grep' or 'awk', ensuring comprehensive data acquisition, evidentiary preservation, and forensic analysis in digital forensics examinations involving complex data recovery tasks, evidence reconstruction efforts, or investigative analysis of electronic data stored on Android or iOS platforms, enhancing forensic capabilities and supporting effective incident response in cases involving digital evidence recovery, data breach investigations, or cybersecurity incidents affecting mobile device usage and electronic data security.

In summary, the benefits of logical extraction in digital forensics include non-invasive data acquisition, scalability, and efficiency in retrieving digital evidence from Android or iOS devices using command-line tools and specialized software, while limitations include dependency on device accessibility, administrative privileges, data fragmentation, and technical challenges impacting the reliability and completeness of extracted data sets retrieved from mobile platforms, requiring forensic analysts to deploy advanced techniques and error-checking procedures to ensure data integrity and evidentiary value in legal proceedings or investigative reports concerning electronic data and digital forensics examinations.

## Chapter 2: Tools and Methods for Logical Acquisition

Popular forensic tools for logical extraction play a crucial role in digital investigations, offering specialized capabilities and command-line interfaces that facilitate the retrieval of user-generated content, application data, and system files from electronic devices while preserving evidentiary integrity and compliance with legal requirements. Tools such as 'Cellebrite UFED', widely used in law enforcement and corporate investigations, enable forensic analysts to initiate logical extraction processes on mobile devices, retrieve text messages, call logs, photos, and application data using commands tailored for specific device models and operating systems, ensuring comprehensive data acquisition and forensic analysis in cases involving digital evidence recovery and evidentiary presentation.

Another prominent tool in the forensic arsenal is 'XRY' by MSAB, which supports logical extraction of data from Android and iOS devices using command-line utilities and proprietary software interfaces designed for forensic analysis of multimedia files, social media interactions, and GPS location data retrieved from mobile devices, enabling analysts to gather digital evidence, reconstruct timelines, and conduct investigative analysis using commands like 'xry extract' or 'xry report', ensuring accurate data extraction and evidentiary preservation in legal proceedings or regulatory investigations concerning electronic data stored on smartphones and tablets.

Furthermore, 'Oxygen Forensic Detective' provides forensic analysts with advanced capabilities for logical extraction of data from Android and iOS devices using command-line tools such as 'oxygen extract' or 'oxygen analyze', facilitating the retrieval of user-generated content, application data, and system files from mobile devices for forensic examination and evidentiary presentation in criminal cases, civil disputes, or regulatory compliance matters involving electronic data recovery and digital evidence preservation.

Moreover, 'MOBILedit Forensic Express' offers forensic investigators a comprehensive toolkit for logical extraction of data from Android and iOS devices using command-line interfaces and proprietary software modules designed for data acquisition, analysis, and reporting in digital forensics examinations, enabling analysts to extract call logs, SMS messages, photos, and application-specific data using commands like 'mobiledit export' or 'mobiledit analyze', ensuring forensic integrity and evidentiary reliability in investigations involving mobile device usage and electronic data recovery efforts.

Additionally, 'Paraben Device Seizure' provides forensic examiners with specialized tools for logical extraction of data from Android and iOS devices using command-line utilities and graphical user interfaces (GUIs) designed for data acquisition, file system analysis, and data carving operations in digital forensics examinations, enabling analysts to retrieve deleted files, recover encrypted data, and reconstruct digital evidence using commands like 'ds acquire' or 'ds analyze', supporting comprehensive forensic analysis and evidentiary presentation in legal proceedings or regulatory investigations involving electronic data stored on smartphones and tablets.

Furthermore, 'Andriller' offers forensic analysts an open-source toolkit for logical extraction of data from Android devices using command-line interfaces and forensic modules designed for data recovery, SQLite database analysis, and multimedia file extraction in digital forensics examinations, enabling analysts to extract SMS messages, call logs, and application data using commands like 'andriller extract' or 'andriller analyze', ensuring forensic accuracy and evidentiary integrity in investigations involving mobile device usage and electronic data recovery tasks.

Moreover, 'Elcomsoft iOS Forensic Toolkit' provides forensic examiners with specialized capabilities for logical extraction of data from iOS devices using command-line utilities and forensic methods tailored for data acquisition, file system analysis, and iCloud synchronization in digital forensics examinations, enabling analysts to retrieve photos, videos, and application-specific data using commands like 'elcomsoft extract' or 'elcomsoft analyze', supporting forensic integrity and evidentiary reliability in investigations involving digital evidence recovery and electronic data preservation.

Additionally, 'Celebrite Physical Analyzer' offers forensic investigators an advanced toolkit for logical extraction of data from Android and iOS devices using command-line interfaces and forensic algorithms designed for data recovery, file system analysis, and multimedia file extraction in digital forensics examinations, enabling analysts to extract geolocation data, social media interactions, and cloud storage files using commands like 'celebrite extract' or 'celebrite analyze', ensuring comprehensive forensic analysis and evidentiary presentation in legal proceedings or regulatory investigations concerning electronic data stored on mobile devices.

In summary, the use of popular forensic tools for logical extraction in digital investigations enables forensic analysts to retrieve user-generated content, application data, and system files from Android and iOS devices using command-line interfaces and proprietary software modules, ensuring comprehensive data acquisition, forensic integrity, and evidentiary reliability in cases involving digital evidence recovery and electronic data preservation efforts in law enforcement, corporate investigations, and regulatory compliance matters. Manual methods for logical acquisition in digital forensics involve systematic approaches and techniques used by forensic analysts to retrieve data from electronic devices without altering the original content or compromising evidentiary integrity, relying on procedural methodologies and command-line tools to initiate data extraction processes and ensure compliance with legal and regulatory requirements governing digital evidence handling and chain of custody procedures in forensic examinations and investigative activities involving mobile devices, smartphones, and tablets.

One of the fundamental manual methods for logical acquisition is the use of 'adb' (Android Debug Bridge) commands to establish a connection between the forensic workstation and an Android device, enabling forensic analysts to retrieve user-generated content, application data, and system files using commands such as 'adb pull' to extract specific directories or files from the device's file system, facilitating forensic analysis and data recovery efforts in cases involving criminal investigations, civil litigation, or regulatory compliance issues affecting digital evidence and electronic data stored on mobile platforms.

Moreover, manual methods for logical acquisition encompass the use of 'idevicebackup2' commands to initiate data extraction processes on iOS devices, enabling forensic analysts to retrieve call logs, SMS messages, photos, and application-specific data stored in device backups using commands like 'idevicebackup2 backup' to create forensic backups of iOS devices and 'idevicebackup2 restore' to recover specific data sets from encrypted or password-protected backups, ensuring comprehensive data acquisition and evidentiary preservation in digital forensics examinations involving iPhones, iPads, and other iOS devices.

Furthermore, manual methods for logical acquisition include the use of file system analysis techniques to examine directory structures, file metadata, and file attributes associated with user data and system files stored on Android or iOS devices using command-line utilities such as 'ls' to list directory contents, 'stat' to display file status information, and 'find' to search for specific files or directories containing digital evidence relevant to forensic investigations, supporting forensic analysis and evidentiary presentation in legal proceedings or regulatory investigations concerning electronic data stored on mobile platforms.

Additionally, manual methods for logical acquisition involve the use of data carving techniques to recover deleted files, fragmented data, and corrupted files from Android or iOS devices using command-line tools such as 'foremost' to extract multimedia files, 'scalpel' to recover deleted files based on file signatures, and 'photorec' to recover photos and videos from unallocated disk space or damaged storage media, enabling forensic analysts to reconstruct digital evidence and document forensic findings using manual extraction methods in cases involving data recovery tasks or evidence reconstruction efforts.

Moreover, manual methods for logical acquisition encompass the use of SQLite database analysis techniques to query database tables, extract records, and analyze structured data associated with installed applications, social media interactions, and user activities on Android or iOS devices using command-line utilities such as 'sqlite3' to interact with SQLite databases, 'grep' to search for specific data patterns, and 'awk' to process and manipulate data retrieved from database files, supporting forensic analysis and investigative analysis in cases involving digital evidence recovery and electronic data examination.

Furthermore, manual methods for logical acquisition include the use of network forensic techniques to capture network traffic, monitor data transmissions, and analyze network connections on Android or iOS devices using command-line tools such as 'tcpdump' to capture packets, 'wireshark' to analyze packet captures, and 'netstat' to display network connections, enabling forensic analysts to investigate network-based attacks, data breaches, or suspicious activities affecting mobile device usage and electronic data security in digital forensics examinations involving network forensics and incident response procedures.

Additionally, manual methods for logical acquisition involve the use of hash value verification techniques to calculate checksums, verify data integrity, and validate forensic images acquired from Android or iOS devices using command-line utilities such as 'md5sum' to calculate MD5 hashes, 'sha256sum' to calculate SHA-256 hashes, and 'hashdeep' to compare hash values between original data sources and forensic copies, ensuring data integrity and evidentiary reliability in forensic examinations and investigative analysis involving electronic data and digital evidence recovery tasks.

In summary, manual methods for logical acquisition in digital forensics encompass a range of procedural techniques, command-line tools, and forensic methodologies used by analysts to retrieve and analyze data from Android and iOS devices without altering the original content or compromising evidentiary integrity, ensuring compliance with legal and regulatory requirements governing digital evidence handling and chain of custody procedures in forensic investigations and incident response activities involving mobile device usage and electronic data storage technologies.

## Chapter 3: Extracting Call Logs and Messages

Techniques for extracting call logs in digital forensics involve systematic approaches and command-line tools used by forensic analysts to retrieve detailed records of incoming, outgoing, and missed calls from mobile devices, ensuring comprehensive data acquisition and evidentiary preservation for forensic analysis and investigative reporting in criminal investigations, civil litigation, or regulatory compliance matters concerning electronic communications and telecommunications data stored on smartphones, feature phones, and other mobile devices.

One of the fundamental techniques for extracting call logs from Android devices involves the use of 'adb' (Android Debug Bridge) commands to establish a connection between the forensic workstation and the device, enabling forensic analysts to retrieve call history records using commands like 'adb shell content query -- uri content://call_log/calls' to query the call log content provider and display detailed call records, including phone numbers, timestamps, call durations, and call types, facilitating forensic analysis and data recovery efforts in cases involving call history reconstruction and digital evidence retrieval from Android smartphones and tablets.

Moreover, techniques for extracting call logs from iOS devices include the use of 'ideviceinfo' commands to retrieve device information and 'idevicebackup2' commands to create forensic backups of iOS devices containing call logs, enabling forensic analysts to extract call history records using commands like 'idevicebackup2 info' to display backup information and 'idevicebackup2 restore --system --settings' to recover call logs from encrypted or password-protected backups, ensuring comprehensive data acquisition and evidentiary preservation in digital forensics examinations involving iPhones, iPads, and other iOS devices.

Furthermore, techniques for extracting call logs encompass the use of forensic software tools such as 'Cellebrite UFED', which supports the extraction of call history records from Android and iOS devices using graphical user interfaces (GUIs) and command-line interfaces designed for forensic analysis of telecommunications data, enabling analysts to retrieve detailed call logs, SMS messages, and multimedia content using commands like 'cellebrite extract' or 'cellebrite analyze', ensuring forensic integrity and evidentiary reliability in investigations involving electronic communications and mobile device usage.

Additionally, techniques for extracting call logs involve the use of SQLite database analysis methods to query database tables, extract records, and analyze structured data associated with call history records stored on Android or iOS devices using command-line utilities such as 'sqlite3' to interact with SQLite databases, 'grep' to search for specific data patterns, and 'awk' to process and manipulate data retrieved from database files, supporting forensic analysis and investigative analysis in cases involving telecommunications data recovery and digital evidence examination.

Moreover, techniques for extracting call logs include the use of data carving techniques to recover deleted call history records, fragmented data, and corrupted files from Android or iOS devices using command-line tools such as 'foremost' to extract multimedia files, 'scalpel' to recover deleted files based on file signatures, and 'photorec' to recover photos and videos from unallocated disk space or damaged storage media, enabling forensic analysts to reconstruct call logs and document forensic findings using manual extraction methods in cases involving data recovery tasks or evidence reconstruction efforts.

Additionally, techniques for extracting call logs encompass the use of hash value verification techniques to calculate checksums, verify data integrity, and validate forensic images acquired from Android or iOS devices using command-line utilities such as 'md5sum' to calculate MD5 hashes, 'sha256sum' to calculate SHA-256 hashes, and 'hashdeep' to compare hash values between original data sources and forensic copies, ensuring data integrity and evidentiary reliability in forensic examinations and investigative analysis involving electronic communications and telecommunications data retrieval tasks.

In summary, techniques for extracting call logs in digital forensics encompass a range of procedural methodologies, command-line tools, and forensic techniques used by analysts to retrieve detailed records of incoming, outgoing, and missed calls from Android and iOS devices, ensuring comprehensive data acquisition, forensic integrity, and evidentiary reliability in criminal investigations, civil litigation, or regulatory compliance matters concerning electronic communications and telecommunications data stored on mobile platforms. Methods for retrieving text messages in digital forensics involve specialized techniques and command-line tools used by forensic analysts to extract and analyze SMS (Short Message Service) and MMS (Multimedia Messaging Service) messages from mobile devices, ensuring comprehensive data acquisition and evidentiary preservation for forensic examination and investigative reporting in criminal investigations, civil litigation, or regulatory compliance matters concerning electronic communications stored on smartphones, feature phones, and other mobile devices.

One of the fundamental methods for retrieving text messages from Android devices involves the use of 'adb' (Android Debug Bridge) commands to establish a connection between the forensic workstation and the device, enabling forensic analysts to retrieve SMS and MMS messages using commands like 'adb shell content query --uri content://sms/' to query the SMS content provider and display detailed message records, including message bodies, timestamps, sender and recipient information, facilitating forensic analysis and data recovery efforts in cases involving communication history reconstruction and digital evidence retrieval from Android smartphones and tablets.

Moreover, methods for retrieving text messages from iOS devices include the use of 'ideviceinfo' commands to retrieve device information and 'idevicebackup2' commands to create forensic backups of iOS devices containing text messages, enabling forensic analysts to extract SMS and MMS messages using commands like 'idevicebackup2 info' to display backup information and 'idevicebackup2 restore --system --settings' to recover message records from encrypted or password-protected backups, ensuring comprehensive data acquisition and evidentiary preservation in digital forensics examinations involving iPhones, iPads, and other iOS devices.

Furthermore, methods for retrieving text messages encompass the use of forensic software tools such as 'Cellebrite UFED', which supports the extraction of SMS and MMS message records from Android and iOS devices using graphical user interfaces (GUIs) and command-line interfaces designed for forensic analysis of electronic communications data, enabling analysts to retrieve detailed message content, attachments, and metadata using commands like 'cellebrite extract' or 'cellebrite analyze', ensuring forensic integrity and evidentiary reliability in investigations involving mobile device usage and communication history analysis.

Additionally, methods for retrieving text messages involve the use of SQLite database analysis techniques to query database tables, extract records, and analyze structured data associated with SMS and MMS messages stored on Android or iOS devices using command-line utilities such as 'sqlite3' to interact with SQLite databases, 'grep' to search for specific data patterns, and 'awk' to process and manipulate data retrieved from database files, supporting forensic analysis and investigative analysis in cases involving electronic communications data recovery and digital evidence examination.

Moreover, methods for retrieving text messages include the use of data carving techniques to recover deleted message records, fragmented data, and corrupted files from Android or iOS devices using command-line tools such as 'foremost' to extract multimedia attachments, 'scalpel' to recover deleted files based on file signatures, and 'photorec' to recover photos and videos from unallocated disk space or damaged storage media, enabling forensic analysts to reconstruct message histories and document forensic findings using manual extraction methods in cases involving data recovery tasks or evidence reconstruction efforts.

Furthermore, methods for retrieving text messages encompass the use of hash value verification techniques to calculate checksums, verify data integrity, and validate forensic images acquired from Android or iOS devices using command-line utilities such as 'md5sum' to calculate MD5 hashes, 'sha256sum' to calculate SHA-256 hashes, and 'hashdeep' to compare hash values between original data sources and forensic copies, ensuring data integrity and evidentiary reliability in forensic examinations and investigative analysis involving electronic communications and message data retrieval tasks.

In summary, methods for retrieving text messages in digital forensics encompass a range of procedural methodologies, command-line tools, and forensic techniques used by analysts to extract and analyze SMS and MMS messages from Android and iOS devices, ensuring comprehensive data acquisition, forensic integrity, and evidentiary reliability in criminal investigations, civil litigation, or regulatory compliance matters concerning electronic communications stored on mobile platforms.

## Chapter 4: Analyzing Contacts and Address Book Data

The structure of the iOS contacts database is crucial in digital forensics, as it dictates how contact information is stored, accessed, and managed on Apple devices, offering insights into communication patterns, social networks, and user interactions without altering the original content or compromising evidentiary integrity, relying on procedural methodologies and command-line tools to initiate data extraction processes and ensure compliance with legal and regulatory requirements governing digital evidence handling and chain of custody procedures in forensic examinations and investigative activities involving iPhones, iPads, and other iOS devices.

One fundamental aspect of the structure of the iOS contacts database is its reliance on SQLite, a lightweight relational database management system widely used in iOS applications and the underlying file system, facilitating forensic analysis and data recovery efforts in cases involving criminal investigations, civil litigation, or regulatory compliance issues affecting digital evidence and electronic data stored on mobile platforms, enabling forensic analysts to retrieve contact details, call histories, and SMS messages using commands such as 'sqlite3' to interact with the SQLite database and 'SELECT * FROM ABPerson;' to query the contacts table and display detailed contact records, including names, phone numbers, email addresses, and social media profiles, supporting forensic integrity and evidentiary reliability in investigations involving contact information reconstruction and digital evidence retrieval from iOS devices.

Moreover, the structure of the iOS contacts database includes multiple tables within the SQLite database file, each storing specific categories of contact information, such as 'ABPerson' for individual contact records, 'ABMultiValue' for phone numbers, email addresses, and social media handles associated with each contact, and 'ABGroup' for contact groups or distribution lists created by users, enabling forensic analysts to extract and analyze contact details using commands like 'SELECT * FROM ABMultiValue WHERE property = "com.apple.MobileMe";' to retrieve iCloud-synced contacts or 'SELECT * FROM ABGroup;' to list all contact groups stored in the database, facilitating comprehensive data acquisition and evidentiary preservation in digital forensics examinations involving iPhones, iPads, and other iOS devices.

Furthermore, the structure of the iOS contacts database encompasses encrypted and unencrypted sections within the SQLite database file, with encryption applied to sensitive data fields such as contact notes, birthdays, and addresses using AES-256 encryption algorithms to protect user privacy and confidentiality, ensuring data security and integrity in forensic analysis and investigative reporting in criminal investigations, civil litigation, or regulatory compliance matters concerning electronic communications and telecommunications data stored on mobile platforms, supporting forensic integrity and evidentiary reliability in investigations involving contact information retrieval and digital evidence examination from iOS devices.

Additionally, the structure of the iOS contacts database includes metadata fields associated with each contact record, such as creation dates, modification timestamps, and unique identifiers (UUIDs), enabling forensic analysts to track changes, identify duplicates, and reconstruct contact histories using commands like 'SELECT * FROM ABMetadata;' to query metadata information stored in the SQLite database file and 'grep' to search for specific data patterns or anomalies in contact records, supporting forensic analysis and investigative analysis in cases involving contact information recovery and digital evidence reconstruction efforts using command-line utilities such as 'grep' to search for specific data patterns or anomalies in contact records.

Moreover, the structure of the iOS contacts database involves relational links between tables within the SQLite database file, enabling forensic analysts to establish connections between individual contact records, call histories, SMS messages, and social media interactions using commands like 'JOIN' to perform SQL joins between tables and 'FOREIGN KEY' constraints to enforce referential integrity in relational database design, facilitating comprehensive data acquisition and evidentiary preservation in digital forensics examinations involving iPhones, iPads, and other iOS devices, ensuring forensic integrity and evidentiary reliability in investigations involving contact information retrieval and digital evidence examination from iOS devices. Extracting and analyzing contact groups in digital forensics involves specialized techniques and command-line tools used by forensic analysts to retrieve, examine, and interpret groupings of contacts stored on mobile devices, ensuring comprehensive data acquisition and evidentiary preservation for forensic examination and investigative reporting in criminal investigations, civil litigation, or regulatory compliance matters concerning electronic communications stored on smartphones, feature phones, and other mobile devices.

One fundamental method for extracting and analyzing contact groups from Android devices involves the use of 'adb' (Android Debug Bridge) commands to establish a connection between the forensic workstation and the device, enabling forensic analysts to retrieve contact group information using commands like 'adb shell content query --uri content://contacts/groups/' to query the contacts content provider and display detailed group records, including group names, member contact IDs, and group IDs, facilitating forensic analysis and data recovery efforts in cases involving communication patterns and social network analysis from Android smartphones and tablets.

Moreover, methods for extracting and analyzing contact groups from iOS devices include the use of 'ideviceinfo' commands to retrieve device information and 'idevicebackup2' commands to create forensic backups of iOS devices containing contact group information, enabling forensic analysts to extract group records using commands like 'idevicebackup2 info' to display backup details and 'idevicebackup2 restore --system --settings' to recover group information from encrypted or password-protected backups, ensuring comprehensive data acquisition and evidentiary preservation in digital forensics examinations involving iPhones, iPads, and other iOS devices.

Furthermore, methods for extracting and analyzing contact groups encompass the use of forensic software tools such as 'Cellebrite UFED', which supports the extraction of contact group records from Android and iOS devices using graphical user interfaces (GUIs) and command-line interfaces designed for forensic analysis of electronic communications data, enabling analysts to retrieve detailed group membership, communication history, and social network data using commands like 'cellebrite extract' or 'cellebrite analyze', ensuring forensic integrity and evidentiary reliability in investigations involving mobile device usage and contact group analysis.

Additionally, methods for extracting and analyzing contact groups involve the use of SQLite database analysis techniques to query database tables, extract records, and analyze structured data associated with contact group information stored on Android or iOS devices using command-line utilities such as 'sqlite3' to interact with SQLite databases, 'grep' to search for specific data patterns, and 'awk' to process and manipulate data retrieved from database files, supporting forensic analysis and investigative analysis in cases involving communication patterns and social network reconstruction from mobile platforms.

Moreover, methods for extracting and analyzing contact groups include the use of data carving techniques to recover deleted group records, fragmented data, and corrupted files from Android or iOS devices using command-line tools such as 'foremost' to extract multimedia attachments, 'scalpel' to recover deleted files based on file signatures, and 'photorec' to recover photos and videos from unallocated disk space or damaged storage media, enabling forensic analysts to reconstruct group memberships and document forensic findings using manual extraction methods in cases involving data recovery tasks or evidence reconstruction efforts.

Furthermore, methods for extracting and analyzing contact groups encompass the use of hash value verification techniques to calculate checksums, verify data integrity, and validate forensic images acquired from Android or iOS devices using command-line utilities such as 'md5sum' to calculate MD5 hashes, 'sha256sum' to calculate SHA-256 hashes, and 'hashdeep' to compare hash values between original data sources and forensic copies, ensuring data integrity and evidentiary reliability in forensic examinations and investigative analysis involving electronic communications and social network data retrieval tasks.

In summary, methods for extracting and analyzing contact groups in digital forensics encompass a range of procedural methodologies, command-line tools, and forensic techniques used by analysts to retrieve, examine, and interpret groupings of contacts stored on Android and iOS devices, ensuring comprehensive data acquisition, forensic integrity, and evidentiary reliability in criminal investigations, civil litigation, or regulatory compliance matters concerning electronic communications stored on mobile platforms.

## Chapter 5: Extracting Photos, Videos, and Audio Files

Methods for extracting media files in digital forensics involve specialized techniques and tools used by forensic analysts to retrieve, analyze, and preserve multimedia content stored on various digital devices, ensuring comprehensive data acquisition and evidentiary integrity for investigative purposes in criminal investigations, civil litigation, or regulatory compliance matters involving electronic media stored on smartphones, tablets, computers, and other digital storage devices.

One essential method for extracting media files from Android devices involves using forensic software tools such as 'Autopsy' to conduct file system analysis and extract multimedia content using graphical user interfaces (GUIs) designed for forensic investigations, enabling analysts to navigate directories and recover media files like photos, videos, and audio recordings by navigating through the file system and using built-in tools to recover deleted files or conduct deep file system scans.

Similarly, methods for extracting media files from iOS devices include the use of 'Cellebrite UFED' to perform logical and physical extractions of multimedia content from iPhones and iPads, using command-line interfaces (CLIs) to initiate extraction processes and retrieve media files such as photos, videos, and audio recordings by executing commands like 'cellebrite extract --media' to specify media extraction parameters and 'cellebrite analyze' to review extracted media files in forensic reports.

Furthermore, methods for extracting media files encompass the use of data carving techniques to recover deleted or fragmented multimedia content from Android or iOS devices using command-line tools such as 'foremost' to extract photos and videos based on file signatures, 'scalpel' to recover deleted files from unallocated disk space, and 'photorec' to retrieve multimedia files from damaged storage media or encrypted partitions, enabling forensic analysts to reconstruct media histories and document digital evidence using manual extraction methods in complex data recovery scenarios.

Moreover, methods for extracting media files involve the use of SQLite database analysis techniques to query metadata associated with multimedia content stored on Android or iOS devices using command-line utilities such as 'sqlite3' to interact with database files, 'grep' to search for specific data patterns, and 'awk' to process and manipulate data retrieved from database tables, supporting forensic analysis and investigative analysis in cases involving multimedia content recovery and digital evidence examination from mobile platforms.

Additionally, methods for extracting media files include the use of hash value verification techniques to calculate checksums, verify data integrity, and validate forensic images acquired from Android or iOS devices using command-line utilities such as 'md5sum' to calculate MD5 hashes, 'sha256sum' to calculate SHA-256 hashes, and 'hashdeep' to compare hash values between original data sources and forensic copies, ensuring data integrity and evidentiary reliability in forensic examinations and investigative analysis involving electronic media and multimedia content retrieval tasks.

Furthermore, methods for extracting media files encompass the use of cryptographic decryption techniques to access encrypted multimedia content stored on Android or iOS devices using command-line tools and forensic software solutions designed to decrypt files, recover passwords, and access protected data, enabling analysts to extract multimedia content and analyze encrypted media files by executing commands like 'openssl' to decrypt data using keys or passwords recovered during forensic analysis processes.

In summary, methods for extracting media files in digital forensics encompass a range of procedural methodologies, command-line tools, and forensic techniques used by analysts to retrieve, analyze, and preserve multimedia content stored on Android and iOS devices, ensuring comprehensive data acquisition, forensic integrity, and evidentiary reliability in criminal investigations, civil litigation, or regulatory compliance matters involving electronic media and multimedia content stored on mobile platforms. Analyzing metadata of media files in digital forensics involves employing specialized techniques and tools to extract, interpret, and utilize the metadata associated with images, videos, audio recordings, and other multimedia content stored on various digital devices, ensuring comprehensive data acquisition and evidentiary integrity for investigative purposes in criminal investigations, civil litigation, or regulatory compliance matters concerning electronic media stored on smartphones, tablets, computers, and other digital storage devices.

One crucial method for analyzing metadata of media files involves using forensic software tools such as 'ExifTool' to extract metadata from digital images and videos, enabling forensic analysts to retrieve detailed information about file attributes, camera settings, and geographical coordinates embedded within the media files by executing commands like 'exiftool -a -u -g1 [file path]' to display all metadata tags and 'exiftool -gpslatitude -gpslongitude [file path]' to extract GPS coordinates from image metadata, facilitating forensic analysis and geolocation mapping in investigations involving multimedia content and digital evidence examination.

Similarly, methods for analyzing metadata of media files from Android devices include using 'Android Debug Bridge (adb)' commands to access media databases and extract metadata associated with photos and videos stored on the device, enabling analysts to retrieve file timestamps, location data, and device information by executing commands like 'adb shell dumpsys media.camera' to query camera-related metadata and 'adb pull /data/media/0/DCIM/Camera/[file name]' to download specific media files for offline analysis, supporting forensic integrity and evidentiary reliability in investigations concerning electronic media and multimedia content stored on Android devices.

Furthermore, methods for analyzing metadata of media files encompass the use of 'FFmpeg' command-line tool to extract metadata from audio and video files, enabling forensic analysts to retrieve information about file formats, codecs, creation dates, and playback duration by executing commands like 'ffmpeg -i [file path]' to display detailed stream information and 'ffmpeg -f ffmetadata -i [file path] -hide_banner' to extract metadata tags stored in FFmpeg-compatible format, facilitating forensic analysis and digital evidence examination in cases involving multimedia content and media file metadata analysis.

Moreover, methods for analyzing metadata of media files involve the use of 'MediaInfo' command-line utility to extract technical metadata from audiovisual files, enabling forensic analysts to retrieve information about video resolutions, audio channels, frame rates, and encoding formats by executing commands like 'mediainfo --Output=XML [file path]' to generate XML-formatted metadata reports and 'mediainfo -- Inform="General;%Encoded_Application%" [file path]' to extract specific metadata fields, supporting forensic integrity and evidentiary reliability in investigations involving multimedia content and digital media analysis tasks.

Additionally, methods for analyzing metadata of media files include using 'PhotoRec' command-line tool to recover deleted or corrupted media files and extract metadata associated with recovered images and videos, enabling forensic analysts to reconstruct file attributes, creation timestamps, and device identifiers by executing commands like 'photorec /dev/sda' to initiate data carving process and 'photorec --output [directory path]' to save recovered files and metadata in designated output directory, supporting digital evidence recovery and forensic analysis in cases involving multimedia content and media file metadata examination.

Furthermore, methods for analyzing metadata of media files encompass the use of 'SQLite' database analysis techniques to query metadata stored in media databases on Android or iOS devices, enabling forensic analysts to retrieve information about file attributes, storage locations, and user interactions by executing commands like 'sqlite3 [database file path] SELECT * FROM MediaStore.Video.Media;' to query video metadata table and 'sqlite3 [database file path] SELECT * FROM MediaStore.Images.Media WHERE _data LIKE '%DCIM%';' to search for image metadata entries, facilitating comprehensive data acquisition and evidentiary preservation in digital forensics examinations.

In summary, methods for analyzing metadata of media files in digital forensics encompass a range of procedural methodologies, command-line tools, and forensic techniques used by analysts to extract, interpret, and utilize metadata associated with images, videos, audio recordings, and other multimedia content stored on Android and iOS devices, ensuring comprehensive data acquisition, forensic integrity, and evidentiary reliability in criminal investigations, civil litigation, or regulatory compliance matters involving electronic media and multimedia content analysis.

## Chapter 6: Retrieving Location Data from iOS Devices

GPS data extraction techniques in digital forensics involve specialized methodologies and tools used by forensic analysts to retrieve, analyze, and interpret geographical location information stored on various digital devices, ensuring comprehensive data acquisition and evidentiary integrity for investigative purposes in criminal investigations, civil litigation, or regulatory compliance matters concerning electronic location data stored on smartphones, tablets, GPS devices, and other digital platforms.

One essential method for GPS data extraction involves using forensic software tools such as 'Cellebrite Physical Analyzer' to perform logical and physical extractions of GPS location information from Android and iOS devices, enabling analysts to access GPS data stored in device logs, location databases, and geotagged media files by executing commands like 'cellebrite extract --gps' to specify GPS extraction parameters and 'cellebrite analyze --gps' to review extracted location data in forensic reports, supporting forensic analysis and investigative mapping in cases involving location-based evidence and digital evidence examination.

Similarly, methods for GPS data extraction from Android devices include using 'Android Debug Bridge (adb)' commands to access location databases and retrieve GPS coordinates stored on the device, enabling analysts to extract latitude, longitude, and timestamp information by executing commands like 'adb shell dumpsys location' to query location-related services and 'adb pull /data/misc/location/gps.conf' to download configuration files containing GPS settings, facilitating forensic integrity and evidentiary reliability in investigations concerning electronic location data and geospatial analysis tasks.

Furthermore, methods for GPS data extraction encompass the use of 'ExifTool' command-line tool to extract GPS metadata from digital images and videos, enabling forensic analysts to retrieve geographical coordinates, altitude, and direction information embedded within media files by executing commands like 'exiftool -gpslatitude -gpslongitude -gpsaltitude [file path]' to display GPS metadata tags and 'exiftool -geotag [directory path]' to extract geotagged media files for offline analysis, supporting forensic analysis and geographical mapping in cases involving multimedia content and location-based evidence examination.

Moreover, methods for GPS data extraction involve using 'GPSBabel' command-line utility to convert GPS data between file formats and extract location information from GPS data logs, enabling forensic analysts to process GPS data files using commands like 'gpsbabel -i gpx -f [input file] -o csv -F [output file]' to convert GPX format to CSV format and 'gpsbabel -t -i nmea -f [input file] -o gpx -F [output file]' to convert NMEA format to GPX format, facilitating data interoperability and analytical workflows in digital forensics examinations involving GPS data extraction and geospatial analysis tasks.

Additionally, methods for GPS data extraction include the use of 'SQLite' database analysis techniques to query location databases on Android or iOS devices, enabling forensic analysts to retrieve GPS coordinates, timestamps, and location history by executing commands like 'sqlite3 [database file path] SELECT * FROM LocationManager;' to query location manager database table and 'sqlite3 [database file path] SELECT * FROM LocationProvider WHERE _id=1;' to search for location provider metadata entries, supporting comprehensive data acquisition and evidentiary preservation in digital forensics investigations.

Furthermore, methods for GPS data extraction encompass the use of 'GDAL/OGR' command-line tools to process GPS data files and perform spatial data analysis tasks, enabling forensic analysts to extract location features, calculate distances, and analyze geospatial relationships using commands like 'ogrinfo [file path]' to display file information and 'ogr2ogr -f GeoJSON [output file] [input file]' to convert GPS data to GeoJSON format for mapping and visualization purposes, supporting forensic analysis and investigative mapping in cases involving electronic location data and geospatial analysis techniques.

In summary, methods for GPS data extraction in digital forensics encompass a range of procedural methodologies, command-line tools, and forensic techniques used by analysts to retrieve, analyze, and interpret geographical location information stored on Android and iOS devices, ensuring comprehensive data acquisition, forensic integrity, and evidentiary reliability in criminal investigations, civil litigation, or regulatory compliance matters involving electronic location data and geospatial evidence examination. Analysis of location history in digital forensics involves the systematic examination and interpretation of geographical data trails captured and stored by various digital devices, enabling forensic analysts to reconstruct user movements, establish timelines, and uncover critical insights for investigative purposes in criminal investigations, civil litigation, or regulatory compliance matters concerning electronic location data stored on smartphones, tablets, GPS devices, and other digital platforms.

One essential method for analyzing location history involves using forensic software tools such as 'Cellebrite Physical Analyzer' to extract and analyze location data from Android and iOS devices, enabling analysts to access historical GPS coordinates, timestamps, and location metadata stored in device logs, location databases, and geotagged media files by executing commands like 'cellebrite extract --location' to specify location extraction parameters and 'cellebrite analyze --location' to review extracted location history in forensic reports, supporting forensic analysis and investigative mapping in cases involving location-based evidence and digital evidence examination.

Similarly, methods for analyzing location history from Android devices include using 'Android Debug Bridge (adb)' commands to access location databases and retrieve historical GPS coordinates stored on the device, enabling analysts to extract location trails, timestamp information, and movement patterns by executing commands like 'adb shell dumpsys location' to query location-related services and 'adb pull /data/misc/location/history.xml' to download XML files containing location history data, facilitating forensic integrity and evidentiary reliability in investigations concerning electronic location data and geospatial analysis tasks.

Furthermore, methods for analyzing location history encompass the use of 'Google Takeout' service to obtain location history data from Google accounts associated with Android devices, enabling forensic analysts to download location data in JSON format using web browser interface or command-line tools like 'wget' to initiate data download process and 'unzip' to extract JSON files for offline analysis, supporting forensic analysis and timeline reconstruction in cases involving digital location data and historical movement patterns examination.

Moreover, methods for analyzing location history involve using 'ExifTool' command-line tool to extract GPS metadata from geotagged digital images and videos, enabling forensic analysts to retrieve geographical coordinates, altitude, and direction information embedded within media files by executing commands like 'exiftool -gpslatitude -gpslongitude -gpsaltitude [file path]' to display GPS metadata tags and 'exiftool -geotag [directory path]' to extract geotagged media files for spatial analysis and timeline reconstruction, supporting forensic analysis and evidentiary preservation in investigations involving multimedia content and location-based evidence examination.

Additionally, methods for analyzing location history include using 'SQLite' database analysis techniques to query location databases on Android or iOS devices, enabling forensic analysts to retrieve GPS coordinates, timestamps, and location history by executing commands like 'sqlite3 [database file path] SELECT * FROM LocationManager;' to query location manager database table and 'sqlite3 [database file path] SELECT * FROM LocationProvider WHERE _id=1;' to search for location provider metadata entries, supporting comprehensive data acquisition and evidentiary preservation in digital forensics investigations.

Furthermore, methods for analyzing location history encompass the use of 'GDAL/OGR' command-line tools to process location data files and perform spatial data analysis tasks, enabling forensic analysts to extract location features, calculate distances, and analyze geospatial relationships using commands like 'ogrinfo [file path]' to display file information and 'ogr2ogr -f GeoJSON [output file] [input file]' to convert location data to GeoJSON format for mapping and visualization purposes, supporting forensic analysis and investigative mapping in cases involving electronic location data and geospatial analysis techniques.

In summary, methods for analyzing location history in digital forensics encompass a range of procedural methodologies, command-line tools, and forensic techniques used by analysts to reconstruct user movements, establish timelines, and uncover critical insights from electronic location data stored on Android and iOS devices, ensuring comprehensive data acquisition, forensic integrity, and evidentiary reliability in criminal investigations, civil litigation, or regulatory compliance matters involving location-based evidence and geospatial analysis tasks.

## Chapter 7: Extracting Browser History and Bookmarks

Techniques for retrieving browser history in digital forensics are crucial for uncovering valuable evidence from web browsing activities conducted on various digital devices, providing forensic analysts with insights into user behavior, visited websites, search queries, and timestamps that are pivotal in investigations related to criminal cases, civil disputes, or regulatory inquiries involving electronic evidence stored on smartphones, tablets, computers, and other digital platforms.

One fundamental method for retrieving browser history involves using forensic software tools such as 'Autopsy' to perform logical acquisitions of internet browsing data from digital devices, enabling analysts to extract browser history entries, timestamps, and website URLs stored in browser cache files and history databases by executing commands like 'autopsy -o [case directory]' to open a case and 'analyze -m [module name]' to select a module for browsing history analysis, facilitating comprehensive data retrieval and evidentiary examination in digital forensics investigations.

Similarly, methods for retrieving browser history from Windows devices include using 'Internet Explorer' browser commands to access browsing history stored in index.dat files, enabling analysts to extract visited URLs, timestamps, and cached web content by executing commands like 'type

C:\Users\[Username]\AppData\Local\Microsoft\Windo ws\History\History.IE5\index.dat' to display contents and 'copy C:\Users\[Username]\AppData\Local\Microsoft\Windo ws\History\History.IE5\index.dat [destination path]' to copy index.dat file for offline analysis, supporting forensic integrity and evidentiary reliability in investigations concerning internet browsing activities and digital evidence examination.

Furthermore, methods for retrieving browser history encompass the use of 'SQLite' database queries to access browser history databases on Android or iOS devices, enabling forensic analysts to retrieve URLs, visit dates, and search queries by executing commands like 'sqlite3 [database file path] SELECT * FROM urls;' to query Chrome browser history database and 'sqlite3 [database file path] SELECT * FROM history_items WHERE visit_count > 0;' to search for history items with visit counts, facilitating comprehensive data acquisition and evidentiary preservation in digital forensics investigations.

Moreover, methods for retrieving browser history involve using 'Google Takeout' service to obtain browsing history data from Google accounts associated with Chrome browsers, enabling forensic analysts to download data in JSON format using commands like 'google_takeout --browser --history --format=json' to specify data extraction parameters and 'wget -O takeout.zip [download link]' to initiate data download process, supporting forensic analysis and timeline reconstruction in cases involving digital browser history data and investigative mapping techniques.

Additionally, methods for retrieving browser history include using 'Mozilla Firefox' browser commands to access browsing history stored in places.sqlite files on Windows, Mac, or Linux devices, enabling analysts to extract visited URLs, timestamps, and bookmark entries by executing commands like 'sqlite3 places.sqlite SELECT * FROM moz_places;' to query places table and 'sqlite3 places.sqlite SELECT * FROM moz_historyvisits;' to search for history visit entries, facilitating forensic analysis and evidentiary examination in investigations concerning Firefox browser activities and digital evidence retrieval.

Furthermore, methods for retrieving browser history encompass the use of 'ExifTool' command-line tool to extract metadata from web browser cache files and history databases, enabling forensic analysts to retrieve timestamps, URLs, and visited website information embedded within media files by executing commands like 'exiftool -URL -DateTimeOriginal -CreateDate [file path]' to display metadata tags and 'exiftool -b -URL [file path]' to extract URL data from browser cache files, supporting forensic analysis and evidentiary preservation in investigations involving multimedia content and internet browsing activities examination.

Moreover, methods for retrieving browser history involve using 'GDAL/OGR' command-line tools to process browser history data files and perform spatial data analysis tasks, enabling forensic analysts to extract location features, calculate distances, and analyze web browsing patterns using commands like 'ogrinfo [file path]' to display file information and 'ogr2ogr -f GeoJSON [output file] [input file]' to convert browser history data to GeoJSON format for mapping and visualization purposes, supporting forensic analysis and investigative mapping in cases involving electronic evidence and geospatial analysis techniques.

In summary, techniques for retrieving browser history in digital forensics encompass a range of procedural methodologies, command-line tools, and forensic techniques used by analysts to extract, analyze, and interpret internet browsing activities stored on various digital devices, ensuring comprehensive data retrieval, forensic integrity, and evidentiary reliability in criminal investigations, civil litigation, or regulatory compliance matters involving electronic evidence and web browsing behavior examination. Analyzing bookmark data in digital forensics involves the systematic examination and interpretation of saved web pages, links, and folders stored in web browsers and bookmark management systems on various digital devices, providing forensic analysts with valuable insights into user preferences, frequently accessed websites, and organizational patterns critical for investigative purposes in criminal cases, civil disputes, or regulatory investigations involving electronic evidence retrieved from smartphones, tablets, computers, and other digital platforms.

One fundamental method for analyzing bookmark data includes using forensic software tools such as 'Autopsy' to perform logical acquisitions and analyze bookmark entries from digital devices, enabling analysts to extract bookmark URLs, timestamps, and folder structures stored in browser cache files and bookmark databases by executing commands like 'autopsy -o [case directory]' to open a case and 'analyze -m bookmarks' to select a module for bookmark data analysis, facilitating comprehensive data retrieval and evidentiary examination in digital forensics investigations.

Similarly, methods for analyzing bookmark data from Windows devices involve using 'Internet Explorer' browser commands to access bookmark data stored in Favorites folder directories, enabling analysts to extract bookmark URLs, timestamps, and folder hierarchies by executing commands like 'dir C:\Users\[Username]\Favorites' to display directory contents and 'copy C:\Users\[Username]\Favorites\Bookmarks.html [destination path]' to copy bookmark files for offline analysis, supporting forensic integrity and evidentiary reliability in investigations concerning internet bookmarking activities and digital evidence examination.

Furthermore, methods for analyzing bookmark data encompass the use of 'SQLite' database queries to access bookmark databases on Android or iOS devices, enabling forensic analysts to retrieve URLs, visit dates, and folder categorizations by executing commands like 'sqlite3 [database file path] SELECT * FROM bookmarks;' to query Chrome bookmark database and 'sqlite3 [database file path] SELECT * FROM bookmarks WHERE date_added > [timestamp];' to filter bookmarks by date added, facilitating comprehensive data acquisition and evidentiary preservation in digital forensics investigations.

Moreover, methods for analyzing bookmark data involve using 'Google Takeout' service to obtain bookmark data from Google accounts associated with Chrome browsers, enabling forensic analysts to download data in JSON format using commands like 'google_takeout --browser --bookmarks --format=json' to specify data extraction parameters and 'wget -O takeout.zip [download link]' to initiate data download process, supporting forensic analysis and timeline reconstruction in cases involving digital bookmark data and investigative mapping techniques.

Additionally, methods for analyzing bookmark data include using 'Mozilla Firefox' browser commands to access bookmark data stored in places.sqlite files on Windows, Mac, or Linux devices, enabling analysts to extract bookmark URLs, timestamps, and folder structures by executing commands like 'sqlite3 places.sqlite SELECT * FROM moz_bookmarks;' to query bookmarks table and 'sqlite3 places.sqlite SELECT * FROM moz_bookmarks_folders;' to search for bookmark folder entries, facilitating forensic analysis and evidentiary examination in investigations concerning Firefox bookmarking activities and digital evidence retrieval.

Furthermore, methods for analyzing bookmark data encompass the use of 'ExifTool' command-line tool to extract metadata from web browser bookmark files, enabling forensic analysts to retrieve timestamps, URLs, and folder categorizations embedded within bookmark data by executing commands like 'exiftool -URL -DateTimeOriginal -CreateDate [file path]' to display metadata tags and 'exiftool -b -URL [file path]' to extract URL data from bookmark files, supporting forensic analysis and evidentiary preservation in investigations involving digital bookmarking behavior and multimedia content examination.

Moreover, methods for analyzing bookmark data involve using 'GDAL/OGR' command-line tools to process bookmark data files and perform spatial data analysis tasks, enabling forensic analysts to extract location features, calculate distances, and analyze bookmarking patterns using commands like 'ogrinfo [file path]' to display file information and 'ogr2ogr -f GeoJSON [output file] [input file]' to convert bookmark data to GeoJSON format for mapping and visualization purposes, supporting forensic analysis and investigative mapping in cases involving electronic evidence and geospatial analysis techniques.

In forensic practice, analyzing bookmark data plays a crucial role in reconstructing user browsing habits, identifying relevant websites, and establishing timelines critical for investigative purposes. By employing these techniques and tools, forensic analysts can effectively extract, analyze, and interpret bookmark data from digital devices, ensuring comprehensive data retrieval, forensic integrity, and evidentiary reliability in criminal investigations, civil litigation, or regulatory inquiries involving electronic evidence and web browsing behavior examination.

## Chapter 8: Analyzing Social Media and Messaging Apps

Forensic analysis of social media data is a critical component of digital investigations, focusing on the systematic examination and interpretation of information derived from social networking platforms and online communication channels, enabling forensic analysts to uncover valuable evidence, user interactions, digital footprints, and behavioral patterns crucial for investigative purposes in criminal cases, civil disputes, or regulatory investigations involving electronic evidence retrieved from smartphones, tablets, computers, and other digital platforms.

One fundamental method for forensic analysis of social media data involves using forensic software tools such as 'Cellebrite UFED' to perform logical acquisitions and analyze social media artifacts from digital devices, enabling analysts to extract chat conversations, multimedia files, timestamps, and user profile information by executing commands like 'ufed logical [device path]' to initiate logical acquisition and 'analyze -m socialmedia' to select a module for social media data analysis, facilitating comprehensive data retrieval and evidentiary examination in digital forensics investigations.

Similarly, methods for forensic analysis of social media data from Windows devices include using 'Internet Evidence Finder (IEF)' software to access social media artifacts stored in web browser cache files, enabling analysts to extract chat logs, posted content, and media attachments by executing commands like 'ief [drive path]' to scan for social media artifacts and 'export -pdf [output file path]' to export findings in PDF format for offline analysis, supporting forensic integrity and evidentiary reliability in investigations concerning online communication activities and digital evidence examination.

Furthermore, methods for forensic analysis of social media data encompass the use of 'SQLite' database queries to access social media databases on Android or iOS devices, enabling forensic analysts to retrieve chat messages, media files, and user interactions by executing commands like 'sqlite3 [database file path] SELECT * FROM messages;' to query messaging app databases and 'sqlite3 [database file path] SELECT * FROM posts WHERE date_created > [timestamp];' to filter posts by creation date, facilitating comprehensive data acquisition and evidentiary preservation in digital forensics investigations.

Moreover, methods for forensic analysis of social media data involve using 'Google Takeout' service to obtain social media data from Google accounts associated with platforms like Google+, enabling forensic analysts to download data in JSON format using commands like 'google_takeout --social --messages --format=json' to specify data extraction parameters and 'wget -O takeout.zip [download link]' to initiate data download process, supporting forensic analysis and timeline reconstruction in cases involving digital social media data and investigative mapping techniques.

Additionally, methods for forensic analysis of social media data include using 'Mozilla Firefox' browser commands to access social media artifacts stored in places.sqlite files on Windows, Mac, or Linux devices, enabling analysts to extract chat logs, posted content, and media attachments by executing commands like 'sqlite3 places.sqlite SELECT * FROM moz_social;' to query social media tables and 'sqlite3 places.sqlite SELECT * FROM moz_historyvisits WHERE visit_type > 0;' to search for history visit entries related to social media activities, facilitating forensic analysis and evidentiary examination in investigations concerning Firefox social media interactions and digital evidence retrieval.

Furthermore, methods for forensic analysis of social media data encompass the use of 'ExifTool' command-line tool to extract metadata from multimedia files and social media artifacts, enabling forensic analysts to retrieve timestamps, location tags, and user information embedded within media content by executing commands like 'exiftool -DateTimeOriginal -Location [file path]' to display metadata tags and 'exiftool -b -ThumbnailImage [file path]' to extract thumbnail images from media files, supporting forensic analysis and evidentiary preservation in investigations involving multimedia content and social media activity examination.

Moreover, methods for forensic analysis of social media data involve using 'GDAL/OGR' command-line tools to process social media data files and perform spatial data analysis tasks, enabling forensic analysts to extract location features, analyze geo-tagged posts, and map user interactions using commands like 'ogrinfo [file path]' to display file information and 'ogr2ogr -f GeoJSON [output file] [input file]' to convert social media data to GeoJSON format for mapping and visualization purposes, supporting forensic analysis and investigative mapping in cases involving electronic evidence and geospatial analysis techniques.

In forensic practice, the analysis of social media data plays a crucial role in reconstructing user interactions, identifying relevant content, and establishing timelines critical for investigative purposes. By employing these techniques and tools, forensic analysts can effectively extract, analyze, and interpret social media data from digital devices, ensuring comprehensive data retrieval, forensic integrity, and evidentiary reliability in criminal investigations, civil litigation, or regulatory inquiries involving electronic evidence and online communication behavior examination. Extraction of messaging app conversations in digital forensics involves the systematic retrieval and analysis of text-based communications exchanged through various messaging applications on smartphones, tablets, computers, and other digital devices, providing forensic analysts with critical evidence and insights into user interactions, conversations, multimedia exchanges, and timestamps essential for investigative purposes in criminal cases, civil disputes, or regulatory investigations.

One fundamental method for the extraction of messaging app conversations includes using forensic software tools such as 'Cellebrite UFED' to perform logical acquisitions and analyze messaging app artifacts from digital devices, enabling analysts to extract chat messages, attachments, timestamps, and user profile information by executing commands like 'ufed logical [device path]' to initiate logical acquisition and 'analyze -m messaging' to select a module for messaging app data analysis, facilitating comprehensive data retrieval and evidentiary examination in digital forensics investigations.

Similarly, methods for the extraction of messaging app conversations from Windows devices involve using 'Internet Evidence Finder (IEF)' software to access messaging app artifacts stored in web browser cache files, enabling analysts to extract chat logs, multimedia attachments, and user interactions by executing commands like 'ief [drive path]' to scan for messaging app artifacts and 'export -pdf [output file path]' to export findings in PDF format for offline analysis, supporting forensic integrity and evidentiary reliability in investigations concerning digital communication activities and electronic evidence examination.

Furthermore, methods for the extraction of messaging app conversations encompass the use of 'SQLite' database queries to access messaging app databases on Android or iOS devices, enabling forensic analysts to retrieve chat messages, media files, and user interactions by executing commands like 'sqlite3 [database file path] SELECT * FROM messages;' to query messaging app databases and 'sqlite3 [database file path] SELECT * FROM media WHERE date_created > [timestamp];' to filter media files by creation date, facilitating comprehensive data acquisition and evidentiary preservation in digital forensics investigations.

Moreover, methods for the extraction of messaging app conversations involve using 'Google Takeout' service to obtain messaging app data from Google accounts associated with platforms like Google Hangouts, enabling forensic analysts to download data in JSON format using commands like 'google_takeout -- messaging --conversations --format=json' to specify data extraction parameters and 'wget -O takeout.zip [download link]' to initiate data download process, supporting forensic analysis and timeline reconstruction in cases involving digital messaging data and investigative mapping techniques.

Additionally, methods for the extraction of messaging app conversations include using 'Mozilla Firefox' browser commands to access messaging app artifacts stored in places.sqlite files on Windows, Mac, or Linux devices, enabling analysts to extract chat logs, multimedia attachments, and user interactions by executing commands like 'sqlite3 places.sqlite SELECT * FROM moz_messages;' to query messaging app tables and 'sqlite3 places.sqlite SELECT * FROM moz_attachments WHERE date_added > [timestamp];' to search for attachment entries related to messaging app activities, facilitating forensic analysis and evidentiary examination in investigations concerning Firefox messaging interactions and digital evidence retrieval.

Furthermore, methods for the extraction of messaging app conversations encompass the use of 'ExifTool' command-line tool to extract metadata from multimedia files and messaging app artifacts, enabling forensic analysts to retrieve timestamps, location tags, and user information embedded within media content by executing commands like 'exiftool -DateTimeOriginal -Location [file path]' to display metadata tags and 'exiftool -b -ThumbnailImage [file path]' to extract thumbnail images from media files, supporting forensic analysis and evidentiary preservation in investigations involving multimedia content and messaging app activity examination.

Moreover, methods for the extraction of messaging app conversations involve using 'GDAL/OGR' command-line tools to process messaging app data files and perform spatial data analysis tasks, enabling forensic analysts to extract location features, analyze geo-tagged messages, and map user interactions using commands like 'ogrinfo [file path]' to display file information and 'ogr2ogr -f GeoJSON [output file] [input file]' to convert messaging app data to GeoJSON format for mapping and visualization purposes, supporting forensic analysis and investigative mapping in cases involving electronic evidence and geospatial analysis techniques.

In forensic practice, the extraction of messaging app conversations plays a pivotal role in reconstructing communication threads, identifying key conversations, and establishing timelines crucial for investigative purposes. By employing these techniques and tools, forensic analysts can effectively extract, analyze, and interpret messaging app conversations from digital devices, ensuring comprehensive data retrieval, forensic integrity, and evidentiary reliability in criminal investigations, civil litigation, or regulatory inquiries involving electronic evidence and digital communication behavior examination.

# Chapter 9: Recovering Deleted Data from iOS Devices

Techniques for data recovery in digital forensics encompass a range of methodologies and tools used to retrieve lost, deleted, or corrupted data from storage devices such as hard drives, solid-state drives (SSDs), mobile devices, and other digital media, essential for recovering valuable evidence and information crucial for investigative purposes in criminal cases, civil disputes, or regulatory investigations.

One primary technique for data recovery involves using forensic software tools such as 'EnCase Forensic' to perform comprehensive disk imaging and analysis of storage devices, enabling analysts to recover deleted files, partitions, and fragmented data by executing commands like 'encase acquire [device path]' to initiate disk imaging and 'analyze -r -f [image file]' to perform a file carving analysis, facilitating thorough data recovery and evidentiary examination in digital forensics investigations.

Similarly, methods for data recovery from Windows devices include using 'Recuva' software to scan for deleted files and recover data from hard drives and removable media, enabling analysts to restore documents, photos, and multimedia files by executing commands like 'recuva /scan [drive letter]' to initiate scan for recoverable files and 'recuva /restore [file path]' to recover selected files to a specified location, supporting forensic integrity and evidentiary reliability in investigations concerning digital evidence retrieval and recovery techniques.

Furthermore, techniques for data recovery encompass the use of 'TestDisk' command-line tool to perform partition recovery and repair damaged file systems on Linux or Unix-based devices, enabling forensic analysts to restore lost partitions, recover deleted files, and fix disk boot problems by executing commands like 'testdisk [device path]' to launch the recovery utility and 'write' to save recovered partitions or files, facilitating comprehensive data restoration and evidentiary preservation in digital forensics investigations.

Moreover, techniques for data recovery involve using 'PhotoRec' command-line tool bundled with TestDisk to recover multimedia files and documents from storage devices, enabling analysts to retrieve photos, videos, and documents by executing commands like 'photorec /dev/sda' to specify the device for recovery and 'y' to confirm file recovery options, supporting forensic analysis and evidentiary examination in cases involving multimedia content and digital evidence retrieval techniques.

Additionally, techniques for data recovery encompass the use of 'GetDataBack' software to perform file system reconstruction and recover data from corrupted storage devices, enabling analysts to restore files, folders, and directory structures by executing commands like 'getdataback [device path]' to initiate scan for recoverable data and 'save' to restore selected files to a designated destination, supporting forensic integrity and evidentiary reliability in investigations concerning digital evidence and data recovery methods.

Furthermore, techniques for data recovery involve using 'EaseUS Data Recovery Wizard' software to scan for lost partitions and recover deleted files from macOS devices, enabling analysts to restore documents, emails, and multimedia files by executing commands like 'easeus_recovery -scan [device path]' to initiate scan for recoverable files and 'easeus_recovery -restore [file path]' to recover selected files to a specified location, facilitating comprehensive data restoration and evidentiary preservation in digital forensics investigations.

Moreover, techniques for data recovery encompass the use of 'Disk Drill' software to perform deep scanning and recover data from external storage devices, enabling analysts to retrieve files, photos, and videos by executing commands like 'diskdrill --scan [drive path]' to initiate deep scan for recoverable data and 'diskdrill --recover [file path]' to restore selected files to a designated destination, supporting forensic analysis and evidentiary examination in cases involving digital evidence and data recovery techniques.

In forensic practice, techniques for data recovery play a crucial role in retrieving lost or deleted information, reconstructing file structures, and recovering valuable evidence essential for investigative purposes. By employing these methodologies and tools, forensic analysts can effectively recover, analyze, and interpret data from various storage devices, ensuring comprehensive data retrieval, forensic integrity, and evidentiary reliability in criminal investigations, civil litigation, or regulatory inquiries involving electronic evidence and digital data recovery techniques. Recovering deleted data poses significant challenges in digital forensics, necessitating advanced techniques and tools to overcome obstacles and retrieve valuable evidence crucial for investigative purposes in criminal cases, civil disputes, or regulatory investigations. One of the primary challenges involves the physical and logical destruction of data caused by deliberate actions such as file deletion, formatting of storage media, or the use of secure deletion tools, making it difficult to recover deleted files using traditional methods.

In such cases, forensic analysts often employ specialized software tools like 'EnCase Forensic' to conduct comprehensive disk imaging and analysis, utilizing commands like 'encase recover -d [device path]' to initiate the recovery process and 'analyze -r -f [image file]' to perform in-depth file carving, enabling the reconstruction of deleted files from disk images and unallocated disk space, overcoming challenges associated with intentional data deletion and ensuring comprehensive data retrieval in digital forensics investigations.

Moreover, challenges in recovering deleted data extend to overwritten data sectors where new information has replaced previously stored data, making it challenging to reconstruct original files and retrieve complete information using traditional recovery methods. To address this issue, forensic analysts employ data carving techniques with tools like 'Foremost' to scan disk images and recover fragmented files, executing commands like 'foremost -t all -i [image file]' to specify file types for recovery and 'mv output /path/to/destination' to move recovered files to a designated location, facilitating the recovery of overwritten data and enhancing data retrieval capabilities in forensic examinations.

Additionally, challenges in recovering deleted data include the encryption of storage media or individual files, where data is protected by cryptographic algorithms and decryption keys, making it difficult to access and retrieve information without appropriate credentials or decryption tools. In such scenarios, forensic analysts utilize tools like 'AccessData FTK Imager' to acquire encrypted disk images and execute commands like 'ftkimager [device path]' to create forensic images, collaborating with encryption experts to obtain decryption keys and decrypt protected data, overcoming challenges associated with encrypted data recovery and ensuring the integrity and confidentiality of recovered information in digital forensic investigations.

Furthermore, challenges in recovering deleted data involve the fragmentation of files across storage media, where file segments are dispersed throughout disk sectors, making it challenging to reconstruct complete files and retrieve accurate information using conventional recovery techniques. To address this issue, forensic analysts employ file system analysis tools like 'Autopsy' to examine disk images and execute commands like 'autopsy -o [image file]' to navigate file system structures, reconstruct file fragments, and recover deleted data segments, enabling comprehensive data recovery and evidentiary examination in digital forensic examinations.

Moreover, challenges in recovering deleted data encompass the volatility of digital evidence stored in volatile memory or temporary storage areas, where data is transient and susceptible to loss during system shutdown or device power-off events, making it crucial for forensic analysts to capture volatile data using tools like 'Volatility Framework' to analyze memory dumps and execute commands like 'volatility -f [memory dump]' to identify and recover volatile artifacts, ensuring the preservation and retrieval of critical evidence in volatile memory analysis and digital forensic investigations.

Additionally, challenges in recovering deleted data include the obfuscation of file metadata and timestamps, where malicious actors manipulate file attributes to conceal digital evidence and mislead forensic investigations, requiring analysts to use metadata analysis tools like 'ExifTool' to examine file metadata and execute commands like 'exiftool -All [file path]' to display metadata tags, timestamps, and digital signatures, facilitating the identification and reconstruction of deleted files based on metadata attributes and ensuring the accuracy and reliability of recovered information in digital forensic examinations.

Furthermore, challenges in recovering deleted data involve the complexity of cloud storage environments, where data is distributed across multiple servers and synchronized across devices, making it challenging to access and retrieve deleted files without proper authorization or cloud storage credentials. To address this issue, forensic analysts utilize cloud forensics tools like 'F-Response' to access cloud storage accounts and execute commands like 'f-response -connect [cloud provider]' to establish forensic connections, collaborating with cloud service providers to obtain access logs and retrieve deleted data from cloud storage repositories, ensuring comprehensive data recovery and evidentiary examination in cloud-based forensic investigations.

In forensic practice, challenges in recovering deleted data require innovative approaches and specialized tools to overcome obstacles associated with intentional data deletion, overwritten data sectors, encrypted data protection, file fragmentation, volatile memory analysis, metadata obfuscation, and cloud storage environments. By employing these techniques and tools, forensic analysts can effectively address challenges in recovering deleted data, ensuring comprehensive data retrieval, forensic integrity, and evidentiary reliability in criminal investigations, civil litigation, or regulatory inquiries involving electronic evidence and digital data recovery methodologies.

## Chapter 10: Practical Challenges in Logical Data Extraction

Handling encrypted data in digital forensics presents a formidable challenge, requiring specialized techniques and tools to access, decrypt, and analyze encrypted information crucial for investigative purposes in criminal cases, civil disputes, or regulatory investigations. One of the primary challenges involves encountering full disk encryption (FDE), where entire storage devices such as hard drives or SSDs are encrypted to protect data from unauthorized access or theft, necessitating forensic analysts to use decryption tools and techniques to access encrypted disks and retrieve critical evidence.

To tackle this challenge, forensic analysts utilize software tools like 'BitLocker' to decrypt FDE-protected drives on Windows systems, executing commands like 'manage-bde -unlock [drive letter] -recoverypassword [recovery key]' to unlock BitLocker-encrypted drives using recovery passwords, enabling access to encrypted data and ensuring forensic integrity in digital forensic investigations.

Moreover, handling encrypted data involves encountering file-based encryption (FBE), where individual files or folders are encrypted to safeguard sensitive information from unauthorized disclosure or modification, posing challenges in accessing and recovering encrypted files without decryption keys or access credentials. In such cases, forensic analysts employ decryption tools like 'AES Crypt' to decrypt AES-encrypted files and execute commands like 'aescrypt -d [encrypted file]' to decrypt encrypted files with specified passwords, facilitating file access and evidentiary examination in digital forensic examinations.

Additionally, handling encrypted data encompasses encountering email encryption, where electronic communications are encrypted to secure sensitive messages and attachments from interception or tampering, making it challenging for forensic analysts to access and recover encrypted email content without decryption keys or encryption certificates. To address this issue, analysts utilize email forensics tools like 'MailXaminer' to analyze encrypted email headers and execute commands like 'mailxaminer -decrypt [email message]' to decrypt encrypted email messages using acquired decryption keys, enabling comprehensive email analysis and evidentiary retrieval in digital forensic investigations.

Furthermore, handling encrypted data involves addressing cloud encryption, where data stored in cloud environments is encrypted to protect confidential information from unauthorized access or data breaches, posing challenges in accessing and retrieving encrypted cloud data without proper authorization or cloud storage credentials. In such scenarios, forensic analysts leverage cloud forensics tools like 'AccessData Cloud

Investigator' to access encrypted cloud storage accounts and execute commands like 'cloud-investigator -connect [cloud provider]' to establish forensic connections and retrieve encrypted data from cloud repositories, ensuring comprehensive cloud data analysis and evidentiary examination in cloud-based forensic investigations.

Moreover, handling encrypted data includes dealing with network encryption, where data transmitted over networks is encrypted to prevent eavesdropping or interception by malicious actors, making it difficult for forensic analysts to capture and analyze encrypted network traffic without decryption keys or network monitoring tools. To overcome this challenge, analysts use network forensics tools like 'Wireshark' to capture encrypted network packets and execute commands like 'wireshark -i [interface] -k [key file]' to decrypt captured packets using encryption keys, facilitating network traffic analysis and evidentiary retrieval in network-based forensic examinations.

Additionally, handling encrypted data encompasses encountering mobile device encryption, where data stored on smartphones or tablets is encrypted to protect personal information and sensitive data from unauthorized access or theft, posing challenges in accessing and recovering encrypted data without device passcodes or encryption keys. In such cases, forensic analysts employ mobile forensics tools like 'Cellebrite UFED' to extract encrypted data from mobile devices and execute commands like 'cellebrite -extract [device model]' to acquire encrypted data and recover deleted files, enabling comprehensive mobile device analysis and evidentiary examination in mobile forensic investigations.

Furthermore, handling encrypted data involves addressing the challenges of encrypted database storage, where relational databases are encrypted to secure sensitive information from unauthorized access or database breaches, making it challenging for forensic analysts to access and retrieve encrypted database contents without proper credentials or database encryption keys. To tackle this issue, analysts utilize database forensics tools like 'SQLite Forensic Toolkit' to analyze encrypted database files and execute commands like 'sqliteftk -decrypt [database file]' to decrypt SQLite-encrypted databases, facilitating database analysis and evidentiary retrieval in digital forensic examinations.

In forensic practice, handling encrypted data requires expertise in decryption techniques and proficiency in using specialized tools to access, decrypt, and analyze encrypted information, ensuring comprehensive data retrieval, forensic integrity, and evidentiary reliability in criminal investigations, civil litigation, or regulatory inquiries involving encrypted electronic evidence and digital data recovery methodologies. Dealing with software and hardware limitations is a critical aspect of digital forensics, requiring forensic analysts to navigate various challenges in accessing, extracting, and analyzing electronic evidence from devices and systems with restricted functionalities or capabilities. One significant software limitation encountered in forensic investigations involves proprietary operating systems such as iOS, where stringent security measures and encryption protocols restrict access to device data without specialized tools and techniques. To overcome this, analysts utilize forensic tools like 'Cellebrite UFED' to perform physical extractions from iOS devices, executing commands like 'cellebrite -extract [device model]' to bypass software limitations and retrieve comprehensive device data for evidentiary examination.

Hardware limitations also pose significant challenges in digital forensics, particularly with aging or damaged storage media, where physical defects or mechanical failures hinder data retrieval and analysis processes. In such cases, forensic analysts employ data recovery techniques like 'ddrescue' to create disk images and recover data from faulty hard drives, executing commands like 'ddrescue -r 3 /dev/sda /mnt/image.img /mnt/logfile.log' to perform multiple retries and salvage data from physically impaired storage media, ensuring forensic integrity and evidentiary preservation in data recovery operations.

Moreover, dealing with software limitations extends to encountering password-protected or encrypted files during forensic examinations, where access restrictions prevent analysts from retrieving critical evidence without decryption keys or access credentials. To address this challenge, analysts utilize decryption tools like 'John the Ripper' to perform password cracking and execute commands like 'john -format=raw-md5 hash.txt' to crack MD5 hashed passwords, facilitating access to encrypted files and enabling comprehensive data analysis in digital forensic investigations.

Furthermore, hardware limitations in digital forensics encompass dealing with obsolete or unsupported devices and technologies, where outdated hardware components or discontinued software versions restrict data extraction and compatibility with modern forensic tools and techniques. In such scenarios, forensic analysts leverage legacy forensics tools like 'EnCase Forensic' to perform forensic acquisitions and execute commands like 'encase -acquire /dev/sdb /mnt/destination' to acquire data from legacy storage devices, ensuring compatibility and forensic accessibility in legacy system investigations.

Additionally, dealing with software and hardware limitations includes encountering volatile memory analysis challenges in forensic investigations, where transient data stored in RAM (Random Access Memory) is volatile and susceptible to loss upon device shutdown or power loss. To address this, analysts utilize memory forensics tools like 'Volatility Framework' to capture volatile memory images and execute commands like 'volatility -f memdump.raw imageinfo' to analyze memory contents and extract critical artifacts, facilitating live memory analysis and evidentiary retrieval in volatile memory forensic examinations.

Moreover, dealing with software and hardware limitations involves addressing data fragmentation issues during forensic acquisitions, where fragmented file storage across storage media complicates data retrieval and reconstruction processes. To mitigate this challenge, analysts use forensic imaging tools like 'FTK Imager' to create forensic images and execute commands like 'ftkimager -e [source] [destination]' to capture fragmented data and reconstruct file structures, ensuring data integrity and evidentiary preservation in fragmented data recovery operations.

Furthermore, dealing with software and hardware limitations encompasses navigating mobile device forensics challenges, where restricted access to locked or disabled devices impedes data extraction and forensic analysis efforts. In such cases, analysts employ mobile forensics tools like 'Magnet AXIOM' to bypass device locks and execute commands like 'magnet-axiom -extract [device model]' to acquire data from locked mobile devices, enabling comprehensive mobile forensic analysis and evidentiary examination in mobile device investigations.

Additionally, dealing with software and hardware limitations involves addressing forensic examination challenges in virtualized environments, where virtual machine configurations and hypervisor security measures restrict forensic access to virtualized system data. To overcome this, analysts utilize virtual forensics tools like 'VMware vSphere' to capture virtual machine snapshots and execute commands like 'vmrun -T esxi -u [username] -p [password] snapshot [vmname]' to snapshot virtual machines for forensic analysis, ensuring virtual environment compatibility and evidentiary integrity in virtualized system investigations.

In forensic practice, dealing with software and hardware limitations requires adaptability, expertise in specialized tools and techniques, and meticulous attention to detail to overcome challenges posed by proprietary systems, obsolete technologies, data encryption, volatile memory, data fragmentation, mobile devices, and virtualized environments, ensuring comprehensive electronic evidence retrieval, forensic analysis, and evidentiary examination in digital forensic investigations.

# BOOK 3
## IOS FORENSICS 101
## MASTERING PHYSICAL DATA ACQUISITION

### ROB BOTWRIGHT

# Chapter 1: Introduction to Physical Data Acquisition

Physical imaging plays a pivotal role in forensic investigations, particularly in the realm of digital forensics, where the acquisition and preservation of digital evidence are paramount. The process of physical imaging involves creating a bit-by-bit copy or forensic image of a storage device, such as a hard drive, solid-state drive (SSD), or mobile device, to capture its entire contents including allocated, unallocated, and hidden data sectors. This comprehensive approach ensures that all potential evidence, whether visible or hidden, is captured and preserved intact for forensic examination and analysis.

In digital forensics, the importance of physical imaging lies in its ability to provide a forensic snapshot of the storage device at a specific point in time. This snapshot not only includes user-accessible files and directories but also system files, deleted data remnants, and metadata crucial for reconstructing digital activities and establishing timelines of events. To perform physical imaging effectively, forensic analysts employ specialized tools like 'dd' (data duplicator), which is a command-line utility available in Unix-based systems and widely used for creating bitwise copies of storage devices. For instance, executing the command 'dd if=/dev/sda of=/mnt/forensic_image.dd bs=1M' creates a forensic image of the entire disk 'sda' and saves it as 'forensic_image.dd' in the '/mnt' directory, ensuring a complete and accurate copy of the original device.

The significance of physical imaging extends to its role in preserving the integrity and authenticity of digital evidence. By capturing a forensic image, analysts ensure that the original data remains unaltered during the investigative process, adhering to the principles of forensic soundness and maintaining the chain of custody. This meticulous approach is essential in legal proceedings, where the admissibility of digital evidence often hinges on its integrity and the procedures followed to acquire it. To maintain forensic integrity, analysts may use write-blocking hardware devices or software tools to prevent any alterations to the original storage device during imaging, thereby preserving its evidentiary value and credibility.

Moreover, physical imaging enables forensic analysts to recover deleted or hidden data that may be critical to an investigation. Deleted files, fragments, and remnants often reside in unallocated sectors or slack space within a storage device, inaccessible through traditional file system navigation. Through forensic imaging, these remnants can be captured and reconstructed using specialized data recovery tools and techniques, providing insights into past activities, communications, or illicit behaviors that may be pivotal in uncovering the truth in forensic investigations.

In addition to recovering deleted data, physical imaging supports the analysis of encrypted or password-protected files and partitions. Encrypted data poses a significant challenge in digital forensics due to its unreadable state without decryption keys or passwords. However, by acquiring a forensic image of an encrypted device or partition, analysts can perform offline decryption using forensic decryption tools like 'Encase' or 'AccessData FTK', executing commands or operations within these tools to recover plaintext data from encrypted volumes. This process allows for thorough examination of encrypted files and their contents, facilitating investigative insights without compromising the security or integrity of the original evidence.

Furthermore, physical imaging plays a crucial role in forensic readiness and incident response strategies within organizations and law enforcement agencies. By routinely performing physical acquisitions of digital assets, organizations can establish baseline images of their systems and devices, enabling rapid response and effective mitigation in the event of security incidents or data breaches. This proactive approach ensures that forensic analysts have access to up-to-date forensic images for timely analysis and investigative purposes, enhancing organizational resilience and compliance with regulatory requirements regarding data protection and incident reporting.

Beyond its investigative and legal implications, physical imaging serves as a foundational practice in digital forensics education and training. Forensic practitioners and aspiring analysts learn the intricacies of imaging techniques, including the nuances of capturing volatile memory, acquiring mobile devices, and handling virtualized environments. Practical exercises and simulations often involve using imaging tools and executing commands to replicate real-world scenarios, preparing professionals to navigate diverse forensic challenges and contribute effectively to investigative teams and legal proceedings.

In summary, the importance of physical imaging in digital forensics cannot be overstated. It forms the cornerstone of evidentiary collection, preservation, and analysis, ensuring that digital evidence is captured comprehensively, preserved with integrity, and analyzed meticulously to support investigative outcomes. Through rigorous adherence to imaging procedures, the forensic community upholds standards of forensic soundness, fosters trust in digital evidence, and empowers justice systems worldwide to adjudicate cases with confidence in the reliability and credibility of digital forensic findings. Distinguishing between logical and physical acquisition methods is fundamental in digital forensics, each serving distinct purposes in extracting and analyzing digital evidence from various devices. Logical acquisition involves retrieving data accessible via the operating system and user-level applications without capturing the entire storage media. This method focuses on extracting files, directories, and user-generated content that are actively stored and accessible on the device. For example, using tools like 'dd' to create a forensic image of a storage device provides a bit-by-bit copy of the entire disk or partition, capturing all data including deleted files and unallocated space crucial for comprehensive forensic analysis. In contrast, logical acquisition tools such as 'ADB' (Android Debug Bridge) are used to retrieve specific data from Android devices, enabling analysts to extract information like call logs, SMS messages, and application data using commands like 'adb pull /data/data/com.example.app/files ./' to pull files from the device to a local directory for examination.

Physical acquisition, on the other hand, encompasses capturing a precise duplicate of the storage device, including both allocated and unallocated sectors, system files, and deleted data remnants. This method ensures a comprehensive capture of all data on the device, regardless of its visibility to the operating system or user-level applications. For instance, in iOS forensics, tools like 'GrayKey' or 'Cellebrite UFED' are employed to perform physical acquisitions of iPhones or iPads, utilizing proprietary techniques to bypass device security measures and extract a complete image of the device's storage, which can then be analyzed using forensic software such as 'Autopsy' or 'XRY' for comprehensive data examination and analysis.

One of the key differences between logical and physical acquisition lies in the scope and depth of data captured. Logical acquisition targets specific files and user-generated content accessible via the device's operating system and applications, providing a focused approach to retrieving active data without capturing system-level information or unallocated space. This method is advantageous in scenarios where quick access to user-generated content like documents, photos, and application data is required without the need for lengthy acquisition processes. Conversely, physical acquisition captures a forensic image of the entire storage media, including both visible and hidden data, system files, and deleted data remnants, ensuring a thorough capture of all potential evidence for forensic analysis and reconstruction.

In terms of deployment, logical acquisition methods are often deployed first in digital investigations due to their speed and targeted approach to retrieving specific data types. Analysts initiate logical acquisitions using tools or commands tailored to the device's operating system and manufacturer specifications, executing commands such as 'adb backup -all -apk' on Android devices to create a full backup of all installed applications and shared storage to the connected computer. This command enables the extraction of application data and associated files stored on the device, providing forensic analysts with access to crucial evidence for investigative purposes.

In contrast, physical acquisition methods require specialized tools and techniques capable of creating a complete forensic image of the storage device. For example, in computer forensics, tools like 'FTK Imager' or 'EnCase' are used to acquire forensic images of hard drives or SSDs, employing write-blocking hardware or software to prevent alterations to the original evidence during imaging processes. Similarly, in mobile forensics, physical acquisition tools such as 'Cellebrite UFED' or 'Oxygen Forensic Detective' enable analysts to perform physical acquisitions of smartphones or tablets, using commands or automated workflows to extract a complete image of the device's storage media for subsequent forensic analysis and examination.

Furthermore, the choice between logical and physical acquisition methods depends on various factors, including the nature of the investigation, device type, and legal considerations. Logical acquisition is preferred in situations where rapid access to user-generated content is critical, such as in incident response scenarios or when dealing with unlocked devices where consent is obtained. In contrast, physical acquisition is indispensable in cases requiring a comprehensive capture of all data on the device, including hidden or deleted information that may be crucial to reconstructing digital activities or establishing timelines of events.

Moreover, the depth of analysis possible with physical acquisition surpasses that of logical methods, as it enables forensic analysts to examine metadata, system logs, and unallocated space for forensic artifacts and evidence. This comprehensive approach is essential in investigations involving complex digital environments, encrypted data, or sophisticated data hiding techniques employed by perpetrators to conceal illicit activities. By leveraging both logical and physical acquisition methods strategically, forensic analysts can maximize the breadth and depth of their investigative findings, ensuring a thorough examination of digital evidence and adherence to forensic best practices.

In summary, while logical and physical acquisition methods serve distinct purposes in digital forensics, both play critical roles in extracting, preserving, and analyzing digital evidence from various devices. Understanding the differences between these methods is essential for forensic practitioners to deploy appropriate techniques based on investigative requirements, device characteristics, and legal considerations, thereby ensuring the integrity and admissibility of digital evidence in judicial proceedings and supporting effective forensic investigations worldwide.

## Chapter 2: Tools and Techniques for Physical Imaging

Forensic imaging tools are indispensable in digital investigations, facilitating the acquisition and preservation of digital evidence crucial for forensic analysis and legal proceedings. These tools enable forensic practitioners to create exact copies or images of storage media such as hard drives, SSDs, mobile devices, and other digital storage mediums, ensuring the integrity and authenticity of the captured data throughout the investigative process. One of the widely used forensic imaging tools is 'dd' (disk dump), a command-line utility available in Unix-like operating systems that creates a bit-by-bit copy of a storage device, ensuring a precise duplication of all data, including file systems, partition tables, and unallocated space, using commands like 'sudo dd if=/dev/sda of=image.dd bs=1M' to create an image 'image.dd' of the storage device '/dev/sda' with a block size of 1 megabyte.

Additionally, tools like 'dcfldd' enhance the capabilities of 'dd' by providing additional features such as hashing, which enables forensic analysts to calculate and verify checksums of the acquired images to ensure data integrity throughout the imaging process, employing commands like 'dcfldd if=/dev/sda hash=md5 hashwindow=10M bs=512 of=image.dd' to create an image 'image.dd' of '/dev/sda' with MD5 hashing and a hash window of 10 megabytes and a block size of 512 bytes. Furthermore, commercial forensic imaging tools such as 'EnCase Forensic' and 'FTK Imager' offer advanced features tailored to forensic investigations, including live acquisition capabilities, support for multiple file systems and storage mediums, and integration with forensic analysis platforms to streamline the acquisition and analysis workflow in complex digital environments.

These tools adhere to forensic best practices by employing write-blocking mechanisms to prevent alterations to the original evidence during imaging processes, ensuring the admissibility and reliability of digital evidence in legal proceedings. Moreover, forensic imaging tools play a crucial role in acquiring evidence from diverse digital devices and storage mediums, ranging from traditional desktop computers and servers to mobile devices like smartphones and tablets, employing techniques like logical acquisition to retrieve specific data sets from a device's file system and physical acquisition to capture a comprehensive image of the entire storage media, including hidden and deleted data.

In mobile forensics, tools such as 'Cellebrite UFED' are instrumental in performing physical acquisitions of smartphones and tablets, employing proprietary techniques to bypass device security measures and extract a complete image of the device's storage, which can then be analyzed using forensic software to recover deleted data, examine application artifacts, and reconstruct digital activities, employing techniques like 'ufed' to begin the process of imaging a cell phone. Analysts may also use tools like 'XRY' to perform comprehensive acquisitions of iOS and Android devices, employing techniques such as "ufed". Best practices for creating forensic images are essential in ensuring the integrity, authenticity, and admissibility of digital evidence in forensic investigations. A fundamental principle is to use a write-blocking hardware device or software solution to prevent any modifications to the original storage media during the imaging process, ensuring that the integrity of the evidence is preserved. Tools like Tableau Forensic Bridges are widely employed for this purpose, connecting to the suspect drive and the forensic workstation without altering the data, such as using Tableau T356789iu to connect a drive.

Another critical practice is to document the entire imaging process meticulously, recording details such as the date and time of acquisition, the equipment used, the commands executed, and any observations made during the procedure, ensuring a clear chain of custody for the evidence. This documentation is crucial for maintaining the legal integrity of the acquired images and for providing transparency in investigative processes, which can be initiated with a command like sudo dd if=/dev/sda of=image.dd bs=1M to begin the imaging process.

Furthermore, it's essential to verify the integrity of the forensic image after acquisition by calculating and comparing hash values using algorithms like MD5 or SHA-256, ensuring that the copy matches the original data bit-for-bit. Commands such as md5sum image.dd or sha256sum image.dd can be used for this purpose, providing a checksum of the image file to verify its integrity, and, in turn, its reliability as evidence.

When dealing with networked storage or remote systems, practitioners must ensure secure transmission of data during imaging processes to prevent unauthorized access or data tampering. Using protocols like SSH (Secure Shell) or SCP (Secure Copy Protocol) ensures encrypted communication between the forensic workstation and the remote system, thereby safeguarding the integrity of the acquired images and maintaining confidentiality during transmission, such as initiating a secure copy using scp user@remotehost:/path/to/forensic_image.dd /local/path/.

Moreover, the choice of imaging tool should be based on its compatibility with the target storage media and the ability to handle various file systems and operating systems effectively. Commercial tools like FTK Imager or open-source solutions such as ddrescue offer different functionalities and capabilities, depending on the complexity and specifics of the digital evidence being acquired. For instance, using ddrescue /dev/sda image.dd logfile to recover data from a failing drive, while also logging the process.

In cases where volatile memory (RAM) acquisition is required, specialized tools like Volatility Framework are employed to capture the volatile data from live systems, enabling forensic analysts to retrieve information such as running processes, network connections, and open files, all of which can be initiated using the framework to perform memory analysis.

Lastly, adherence to legal and regulatory guidelines is paramount in forensic imaging practices. Understanding the jurisdiction-specific laws governing digital evidence and ensuring compliance with standards such as ISO/IEC 27037 for guidelines on digital evidence acquisition is crucial for the admissibility of the acquired images in legal proceedings. This compliance ensures that forensic imaging practices maintain the highest standards of integrity, accuracy, and reliability, supporting the investigative process and contributing to the pursuit of justice in digital forensic examinations.

## Chapter 3: Understanding the iOS Secure Enclave

The Secure Enclave plays a pivotal role in the security architecture of Apple devices, particularly iOS devices, serving as a critical component that enhances the protection of sensitive data and cryptographic operations. It is a separate co-processor embedded within the main system-on-chip (SoC) of supported devices, such as iPhone models from iPhone 5s onwards, designed to handle cryptographic operations, secure key management, and other security-related tasks independently from the main processor. This isolation ensures that sensitive information, like cryptographic keys used for Touch ID, Face ID, and other security features, remains protected from potential attacks, and ensuring their secure management and deployment.

One of the primary functionalities of the Secure Enclave is its role in biometric authentication, managing and processing biometric data in a secure environment to verify user identities without exposing sensitive information to the main processor or the operating system, such as using Apple's Face ID to unlock an iPhone. The Secure Enclave ensures that biometric data remains encrypted and is never stored on Apple's servers or backed up to iCloud, maintaining user privacy and confidentiality in compliance with stringent privacy regulations and maintaining a secure connection with the security of the device.

Another critical aspect of the Secure Enclave's functionality is its role in securing cryptographic operations and sensitive data, such as the generation, storage, and handling of encryption keys used for data protection and secure communication, which are pivotal in ensuring the security of communications and transactions in applications that use the iMessage or Apple Pay, such as generating keys for encryption and decryption.

Moreover, the Secure Enclave facilitates the enforcement of hardware-based security policies and ensures the integrity of the boot process through secure boot mechanisms, thereby protecting against unauthorized modifications to the device's firmware and operating system. This is achieved through secure boot and other hardware mechanisms, such as verifying the integrity of the operating system and applications before they are loaded into memory, and ensuring the integrity of the device's hardware and software.

Additionally, the Secure Enclave supports the execution of trusted execution environments (TEEs), such as the execution of trusted applications and processes within a secure environment, such as executing Apple's Wallet app or processing payments using Apple Pay, ensuring that sensitive operations and data remain protected from potentially malicious attacks or software vulnerabilities.

Furthermore, the Secure Enclave enhances the security of data at rest by managing and encrypting the device's file system encryption keys, such as encrypting and decrypting files stored on the device and securing data stored in iCloud or other cloud services, ensuring that data remains protected even if the physical device is lost or stolen. This involves the generation, storage, and management of keys used for file system encryption, and ensuring that data remains protected even if the physical device is lost or stolen.

In summary, the Secure Enclave plays a crucial role in the security architecture of Apple devices, ensuring the protection of sensitive data, cryptographic operations, and biometric authentication, while maintaining user privacy and confidentiality. Its design and functionality are instrumental in enabling secure biometric authentication, managing cryptographic keys, enforcing hardware-based security policies, and securing data at rest, making it an essential component in safeguarding the integrity and security of iOS devices. Security features and protections provided by modern operating systems and devices are essential components in safeguarding digital information and ensuring user privacy. In the context of iOS, Apple has implemented a robust array of security measures designed to mitigate threats, protect sensitive data, and maintain the integrity of the operating system and user interactions. These security features span both hardware and software layers, incorporating mechanisms that defend against various attack vectors and vulnerabilities that could compromise device security.

At the forefront of iOS security is the hardware-based Secure Enclave, a dedicated co-processor embedded within the device's SoC (System on Chip), responsible for managing sensitive operations like cryptographic processing and biometric data. To manage and protect sensitive data such as cryptographic keys used for encryption and authentication, the Secure Enclave utilizes a dedicated microkernel known as SEP (Secure Enclave Processor). This separation ensures that sensitive operations are isolated from the main processor and operating system, minimizing the risk of unauthorized access or tampering.

For securing user authentication, iOS leverages biometric authentication methods such as Face ID and Touch ID. Face ID, for instance, utilizes facial recognition technology powered by the TrueDepth camera system, which captures and analyzes facial data to authenticate users securely. To enable Face ID, administrators or users must first configure their device by navigating to the Settings app and selecting "Face ID & Passcode," followed by tapping "Enroll Face." This process prompts the device to capture a detailed scan of the user's face, which is then securely stored within the Secure Enclave for subsequent authentication attempts.

In addition to biometric authentication, iOS incorporates strong passcode policies to further fortify device security. Users can set complex passcodes by navigating to the

"Passcode & Face ID" settings within the Settings app and selecting "Change Passcode." From there, users can opt for a custom alphanumeric passcode to enhance device protection further. The complexity and uniqueness of the passcode bolster the overall security posture of the device, thwarting brute-force attacks and unauthorized access attempts.

To safeguard sensitive user data stored on iOS devices, Apple implements robust encryption mechanisms across various data types and storage locations. For instance, iOS employs AES-256 encryption to protect data stored locally on the device, such as photos, videos, documents, and application data. Encryption keys utilized for data protection are securely managed by the Secure Enclave, ensuring that even if physical access to the device is compromised, unauthorized entities cannot decipher encrypted data without the corresponding decryption keys.

Furthermore, iOS devices benefit from sandboxing, a security mechanism that restricts the capabilities of individual applications to prevent them from accessing sensitive system resources or data belonging to other apps. Each iOS application runs within its designated sandbox environment, isolated from other applications and the underlying operating system. This isolation mitigates the risk of malicious applications compromising device security or accessing unauthorized data, thereby bolstering overall system integrity. For enterprise environments and organizations deploying iOS devices, Apple offers a suite of management tools and security features under the umbrella of Apple Business Manager and Mobile Device Management (MDM) solutions. These tools enable administrators to enforce security policies, configure device settings, and remotely manage and monitor iOS devices deployed across the organization. To initiate device management and security policy enforcement, administrators can utilize MDM commands such as "mdmclient" to establish secure connections with enrolled devices and deploy configurations remotely.

Moreover, iOS incorporates built-in measures to defend against malware and malicious software threats. The App Store ecosystem employs stringent app review processes and code signing requirements to ensure that applications distributed through the App Store are vetted for security vulnerabilities and adhere to Apple's strict guidelines. Additionally, iOS devices benefit from runtime protections such as Address Space Layout Randomization (ASLR) and Data Execution Prevention (DEP), which mitigate the risk of memory-based attacks and buffer overflow exploits.

In summary, the security features and protections provided by iOS devices are pivotal in safeguarding user data, mitigating security risks, and maintaining the integrity of the operating system. From hardware-based security measures like the Secure Enclave and biometric authentication to software-based encryption, sandboxing, and enterprise-grade management tools, iOS offers a comprehensive security framework designed to address modern-day threats and ensure user privacy in an increasingly interconnected digital landscape.

**Chapter 4: Advanced File System Analysis Techniques**

In-depth analysis of iOS file system structures is a crucial endeavor for forensic investigators, IT administrators, and developers alike, providing foundational insights into how data is stored, organized, and managed within Apple's mobile operating system. At the heart of iOS file system architecture lies a hierarchical directory structure rooted in Unix principles, where each directory serves a specific purpose and houses various files and subdirectories essential for the system's operation and application data storage. To navigate through the iOS file system and explore its intricacies, analysts can utilize command-line interface (CLI) commands such as "ls" to list directory contents, "cd" to change directories, and "pwd" to display the current directory path, enabling a comprehensive examination of file organization and structure.

iOS file system is predominantly based on the Apple File System (APFS), which replaced the earlier Hierarchical File System Plus (HFS+) due to its enhanced capabilities in managing flash storage and providing advanced features like snapshots, cloning, and native encryption. APFS partitions the storage into containers, each capable of hosting multiple volumes, thereby optimizing storage utilization and improving data integrity and performance. By employing the "diskutil" command in the CLI, analysts can interact with APFS containers and volumes, create new volumes, resize existing ones, or verify disk integrity, ensuring robust data management practices in forensic investigations and everyday system maintenance tasks.

The root directory "/" serves as the starting point for navigating the iOS file system, housing essential directories such as "/System" and "/Library" that contain critical system files, binaries, and configurations necessary for the device's operation. Analysts can explore these directories using commands like "ls /System" to list system files or "ls /Library" to examine library files and configurations, providing insights into system-level functionalities and dependencies crucial for forensic examinations and troubleshooting scenarios.

One of the pivotal aspects of iOS file system analysis is understanding the role of sandboxing, where each application operates within its designated sandbox directory located at "/var/mobile/Applications". Sandbox directories are uniquely identified by Universally Unique Identifiers (UUIDs) and encapsulate an application's data, preferences, and temporary files, ensuring data isolation and security between applications. By navigating to these directories using CLI commands like "cd /var/mobile/Applications" followed by "ls" to list installed applications, analysts can investigate application-specific data, assess privacy implications, and identify potential security vulnerabilities.

Moreover, iOS file system structures include symbolic links, which serve as pointers to files or directories located elsewhere within the file system hierarchy. Symbolic links are created using the "ln -s" command followed by the source file or directory and the destination path of the symbolic link, facilitating efficient file management and enabling applications to access resources stored in different locations seamlessly. Analysts can utilize commands like "ln -s /path/to/source /path/to/destination" to create symbolic links and "ls -l" to display detailed information about symbolic links, including their target and permissions.

In forensic investigations, analyzing iOS file system metadata provides valuable insights into file attributes such as creation dates, modification timestamps, file size, and file type identifiers, facilitating timeline reconstruction and data validation processes. CLI commands like "ls -l" and "stat" enable analysts to retrieve detailed metadata information, aiding in the identification of file ownership, access permissions, and forensic artifacts essential for establishing evidentiary integrity and reconstructing digital timelines accurately.

Furthermore, iOS file system analysis extends to examining file compression and encryption techniques utilized to optimize storage efficiency and safeguard sensitive information. Compression utilities like "zip" and "gzip" enable analysts to compress files and directories, reducing storage footprint and enhancing data transfer speeds, while encryption mechanisms such as FileVault and Data Protection ensure data confidentiality and protection against unauthorized access. Analysts can employ CLI commands like "zip -r archive.zip directory" for recursive compression or "openssl enc -aes-256-cbc -in file.txt -out file.enc" for file encryption, adhering to best practices in data security and privacy.

Additionally, iOS file system structures encompass temporary directories and cache files located within "/var/mobile/Library/Caches" and "/private/var/tmp", containing transient data generated by applications during runtime. These directories may store artifacts relevant to user activities, including cached images, web browsing data, and application logs, which analysts can examine using CLI commands such as "cd /var/mobile/Library/Caches" followed by "ls" to enumerate cached content and investigate potential forensic leads.

In summary, an in-depth analysis of iOS file system structures through CLI commands and forensic techniques provides invaluable insights into data storage, organization, and security mechanisms inherent to Apple's mobile ecosystem. By navigating directory hierarchies, examining metadata attributes, and understanding file system dependencies, analysts can effectively conduct forensic investigations, mitigate security risks, and optimize system performance, ensuring comprehensive data management practices and adherence to digital forensic protocols in iOS environments. File carving and reconstruction techniques are fundamental to digital forensics, enabling investigators to recover fragmented or deleted files from storage media without relying on filesystem metadata. This process is crucial in scenarios where file headers, footers, or other structural information are missing or corrupted, requiring specialized tools and methodologies to identify and reconstruct file content accurately. One of the primary techniques employed in file carving is pattern matching, where forensic tools scan raw disk images or memory dumps using predefined signatures or byte sequences to locate file boundaries and extract data. Tools such as "scalpel" and "foremost" utilize signature files containing patterns specific to file types like images, documents, and archives, facilitating automated file recovery from unallocated disk space or fragmented data clusters.

Another effective file carving technique involves header/footer analysis, focusing on identifying unique file signatures or magic numbers located at the beginning or end of file structures. By analyzing these signatures using commands like "xxd" or "hexdump" to examine raw data, investigators can determine file boundaries and extract content accordingly. For example, to identify JPEG file headers, analysts can use "xxd -l 10 -g 1 file.dd" to inspect the first ten bytes of a disk image and search for the characteristic "FF D8" marker indicative of JPEG files, guiding subsequent extraction efforts.

Furthermore, entropy analysis is employed to distinguish between different file types based on their data randomness or entropy levels. High-entropy files like encrypted data or compressed archives exhibit more uniform byte distribution compared to low-entropy files such as text documents or uncompressed images. Tools like "binwalk" leverage entropy analysis to detect and extract embedded files within binary data streams or file formats like firmware images, assisting in the reconstruction of concealed or obfuscated content crucial for forensic examinations.

In addition to automated techniques, manual file carving methodologies involve hexadecimal inspection and data carving based on forensic expertise and investigative intuition. Analysts can use CLI commands such as "hexdump -C" to examine hexadecimal representations of data blocks and identify potential file structures or artifacts embedded within unallocated disk sectors. This approach enables precise file reconstruction by manually delineating file boundaries and extracting data segments aligned with specific file type specifications, ensuring accuracy in recovering fragmented or partially overwritten files during forensic investigations.

Moreover, file carving encompasses sequential and non-sequential extraction methods to recover files stored in contiguous or fragmented disk sectors. Sequential extraction involves reading consecutive disk sectors and reconstructing files based on their sequential allocation within the file system, utilizing commands like "dd" to copy data blocks from specified disk offsets. Conversely, non-sequential extraction techniques such as cluster-based carving reconstruct files dispersed across fragmented disk clusters by traversing file system structures and assembling data fragments using forensic tools like "Scalpel" with specified configuration files.

Forensic analysts also employ hashing techniques such as MD5 or SHA-256 to verify file integrity during the carving and reconstruction process. By calculating hash values for extracted files and comparing them with known hashes from reference sources, investigators can validate data consistency and detect alterations or tampering attempts, ensuring the reliability and authenticity of recovered evidence in legal proceedings. CLI commands like "md5sum" or "sha256sum" compute hash values for extracted files, providing cryptographic checksums for verification purposes and maintaining forensic chain of custody.

Furthermore, metadata analysis complements file carving techniques by examining timestamp information, file attributes, and ownership details associated with recovered files. Tools like "exiftool" enable analysts to extract and parse metadata embedded within images, documents, or multimedia files, revealing crucial investigative leads such as creation dates, device identifiers, and user interactions.

By leveraging CLI commands such as "exiftool -a -u -g1 file.jpg" to display all metadata groups for a JPEG image, investigators can reconstruct digital timelines, ascertain file provenance, and establish contextual relevance in forensic examinations.

In summary, file carving and reconstruction techniques represent essential methodologies in digital forensics, enabling investigators to recover, reconstruct, and validate file content from raw disk images or fragmented data clusters. Through pattern matching, header/footer analysis, entropy assessment, and manual hexadecimal inspection, forensic analysts employ CLI commands and specialized tools to extract files, verify integrity, and uncover hidden or deleted data crucial for investigative insights and evidentiary preservation. These techniques uphold forensic best practices, ensuring thorough data recovery and analysis in diverse forensic scenarios, from criminal investigations to corporate incident response and cybersecurity assessments.

## Chapter 5: Decrypting Encrypted Data on iOS Devices

Decrypting file-level encryption is a critical task in digital forensics, essential for accessing and analyzing encrypted data stored on devices or within files. This process involves various methods and techniques designed to decipher cryptographic protections applied to files, ensuring that forensic investigators can retrieve valuable evidence without altering the original data integrity. One of the primary approaches to decrypting file-level encryption is through cryptographic key recovery, where forensic analysts attempt to acquire or reconstruct encryption keys used to encrypt the data. This method is particularly effective when encryption keys are stored insecurely or when key recovery tools can exploit vulnerabilities in encryption implementations to extract keys. Tools such as "AESKeyFinder" can be deployed to search memory dumps or disk images for cryptographic keys, employing commands like "aeskeyfind" followed by the path to the image file to identify potential encryption keys embedded within system memory or storage media.

Additionally, brute-force attacks represent another method for decrypting file-level encryption, involving systematic trial-and-error attempts to guess the correct decryption key by testing all possible combinations until the correct one is found. This technique is resource-intensive and time-consuming but can be effective against weak or poorly implemented encryption schemes where keys are short or lack entropy. CLI commands such as "john" or "hashcat" are commonly used in forensic investigations to initiate brute-force attacks against hashed passwords or encryption keys, specifying parameters like character sets, length constraints, and hashing algorithms to optimize key recovery efforts and accelerate decryption processes.

Moreover, dictionary attacks are employed to decrypt file-level encryption by leveraging precompiled lists of commonly used passwords or phrases that may serve as encryption keys. These attacks are more targeted and efficient than brute-force methods, focusing on likely passwords based on linguistic patterns, user behaviors, or known vulnerabilities in password selection practices. Forensic tools like "hashcat" support dictionary attacks against hashed passwords, utilizing commands such as "hashcat -m 0 -a 0 hash.txt rockyou.txt" to attempt decryption using a dictionary file ("rockyou.txt") against a specified hash file ("hash.txt"), enabling rapid identification of weak or predictable encryption keys.

Furthermore, rainbow table attacks facilitate decryption by precomputing hash values for all possible plaintext inputs and storing them in a lookup table format, enabling rapid retrieval of plaintext equivalents for encrypted data. These tables significantly accelerate decryption processes for specific encryption algorithms and hash functions, leveraging CLI commands like "rtgen" or "rainbowcrack" to generate and utilize rainbow tables against hashed data sets, expediting forensic investigations by providing instant access to plaintext content without requiring extensive computational resources.

In addition to cryptographic attacks, side-channel attacks exploit unintended information leakage from physical devices or cryptographic implementations to deduce encryption keys indirectly. Techniques such as timing analysis, power analysis, or electromagnetic emanation analysis can reveal patterns or characteristics related to encryption operations, aiding in the reconstruction or inference of encryption keys used to protect file-level data. While these methods are sophisticated and require specialized equipment and expertise, they represent viable approaches for decrypting file-level encryption in targeted forensic scenarios where conventional cryptographic attacks may be impractical or ineffective.

Moreover, plaintext recovery techniques involve searching for unencrypted copies or remnants of encrypted files in unallocated disk space, memory dumps, or temporary storage areas where plaintext data may have been inadvertently retained or stored during encryption or decryption processes. Forensic analysts utilize CLI commands such as "grep" or "strings" to scan disk images or memory captures for recognizable plaintext strings or file headers, facilitating the identification and extraction of unencrypted content embedded within encrypted files, providing valuable insights into digital artifacts or evidence pertinent to forensic investigations.

Additionally, collaborative decryption efforts involve leveraging community-sourced resources, online forums, or collaborative platforms to share encrypted data samples, encryption keys, or decryption strategies among forensic professionals and researchers. These collaborative initiatives enhance decryption capabilities by pooling collective knowledge, expertise, and computational resources to tackle complex encryption challenges and overcome technical barriers associated with file-level encryption in digital forensics.

Furthermore, advanced cryptographic techniques such as differential cryptanalysis, chosen plaintext attacks, or meet-in-the-middle attacks are employed to exploit weaknesses in encryption algorithms or protocols, facilitating more efficient decryption of file-level encryption in targeted forensic investigations. CLI commands and specialized tools like "Cryptool" or "IDA Pro" are utilized to implement and execute these advanced cryptographic techniques, enabling forensic analysts to assess encryption strength, identify vulnerabilities, and devise effective decryption strategies tailored to specific encryption implementations or security architectures.

In summary, decrypting file-level encryption in digital forensics involves employing a diverse array of methodologies, tools, and techniques tailored to the unique characteristics and challenges posed by encrypted data. From cryptographic key recovery and brute-force attacks to dictionary attacks, rainbow table methods, and advanced cryptographic analysis, forensic investigators utilize CLI commands and specialized tools to unlock encrypted files, retrieve valuable evidence, and support comprehensive forensic examinations without compromising data integrity or confidentiality. These methods underscore the importance of continual research, collaboration, and innovation in developing effective decryption strategies to address evolving encryption technologies and encryption standards in contemporary digital environments. Breaking into encrypted databases is a complex task that requires specialized knowledge and tools in digital forensics. Encrypted databases are designed to protect sensitive information from unauthorized access, using cryptographic algorithms to encode data in such a way that only authorized parties with the correct decryption key can access it. However, in forensic investigations, there are legitimate reasons to gain access to encrypted databases to retrieve crucial evidence for legal proceedings or investigative purposes.

To begin with, one of the fundamental techniques used in breaking into encrypted databases involves identifying the type of encryption algorithm used and attempting to obtain the encryption key. In many cases, databases use standard encryption algorithms such as AES (Advanced Encryption Standard) or RSA (Rivest–

Shamir–Adleman), which are widely recognized for their robust security.

For instance, if an investigator has access to the server where the database is hosted, they may try to locate configuration files or environment variables that store the encryption keys. In a Unix/Linux environment, one might use commands such as `grep` or `find` to search for keywords like "encryption_key" or "AES_key" within configuration files or source code.

Another approach involves leveraging cryptographic weaknesses or vulnerabilities in the implementation of encryption algorithms or protocols. For example, if a database system has not been updated to patch known vulnerabilities, an attacker may exploit these weaknesses using specific techniques like SQL injection or buffer overflow attacks to gain unauthorized access to the encryption keys or decrypted data.

Furthermore, brute-force attacks represent another method used to break into encrypted databases, although this approach is typically resource-intensive and time-consuming. Brute-forcing involves systematically trying all possible combinations of keys until the correct one is found. For example, in a scenario where an encryption key is a 128-bit AES key, there are $2^{128}$ possible combinations, making brute-forcing impractical without substantial computing power and time.

Moreover, social engineering techniques can sometimes be used to manipulate individuals with authorized access to encrypted databases into divulging their credentials or encryption keys. This could be achieved through phishing attacks, pretexting, or other forms of deception designed to exploit human vulnerabilities rather than technical weaknesses.

In addition to these methods, forensic analysts often employ specialized tools and software designed specifically for cryptographic analysis and decryption tasks. For instance, tools like `John the Ripper` or `Hashcat` are commonly used for password cracking and can be adapted to work on encryption keys as well. These tools utilize various techniques such as dictionary attacks, brute-force attacks, and rainbow tables to crack passwords and encryption keys.

Moreover, it's crucial for forensic analysts to follow legal and ethical guidelines when attempting to break into encrypted databases. Obtaining proper authorization or warrants, depending on the jurisdiction, is essential to ensure that any evidence gathered is admissible in court and obtained through lawful means. Violating legal and ethical boundaries in the pursuit of evidence can undermine the credibility of forensic investigations and potentially lead to legal consequences for investigators.

Furthermore, it's important to note that breaking into encrypted databases is often a last resort in forensic investigations, and investigators should exhaust all other avenues of obtaining evidence before resorting to decryption methods. This approach ensures that privacy rights are respected, and investigations are conducted in a thorough and professional manner.

In summary, breaking into encrypted databases requires a combination of technical expertise, specialized tools, and adherence to legal and ethical guidelines. It remains a challenging task in digital forensics, requiring careful consideration of the methods used and the implications for privacy and legal integrity. By employing rigorous methodologies and respecting legal boundaries, forensic analysts can effectively navigate the complexities of encrypted data and contribute valuable insights to investigative processes without compromising ethical standards.

## Chapter 6: Extracting System and Application Logs

Logs play a pivotal role in forensic investigations, serving as invaluable sources of chronological data and evidence that can illuminate the sequence of events leading up to and following a security incident or digital crime. These logs are typically generated by various systems, applications, and devices across networks, capturing crucial details such as user activities, system events, network traffic, and application interactions. For instance, in a Unix/Linux environment, logs are often stored in `/var/log/`, and commands like `grep`, `tail`, or `cat` can be used to analyze their contents.

One of the primary functions of logs in forensic investigations is to establish a timeline of events, providing investigators with a chronological sequence of actions taken by users or systems. This timeline can be instrumental in reconstructing the sequence of an attack, identifying its origin, and understanding the methods used by perpetrators to exploit vulnerabilities or gain unauthorized access. For instance, using the `grep` command in Unix/Linux systems, investigators can filter logs based on specific keywords or timestamps to trace the activities of a suspicious user or process.

Moreover, logs serve as critical evidence in legal proceedings, offering a detailed record of activities that can substantiate or refute allegations of wrongdoing. They provide a forensic trail that links actions to individuals or entities, helping to establish accountability and support the prosecution or defense of cases related to cybercrime, data breaches, or unauthorized access incidents. For example, analyzing web server logs using tools like `awk` or `sed` can reveal patterns of suspicious requests or attempts to exploit vulnerabilities in web applications.

Furthermore, logs contribute to the detection and mitigation of security incidents by enabling real-time monitoring and alerting mechanisms. Security Information and Event Management (SIEM) systems aggregate and analyze logs from multiple sources, allowing organizations to detect anomalies, unauthorized access attempts, malware infections, or other indicators of compromise promptly. Commands such as `tail -f` in Unix/Linux systems enable real-time monitoring of logs, providing immediate visibility into ongoing activities and potential security threats.

In addition to their role in incident response and investigation, logs facilitate compliance with regulatory requirements and industry standards governing data privacy and security. Many regulations, such as the GDPR (General Data Protection Regulation) and PCI DSS (Payment Card Industry Data Security Standard), mandate the collection, retention, and protection of logs to ensure transparency, accountability, and the safeguarding of sensitive information. Compliance audits often require organizations to demonstrate the adequacy of their log management practices and the integrity of log data.

Moreover, logs serve as a tool for performance monitoring and troubleshooting in addition to their forensic and security-related uses. By analyzing system logs, administrators can identify performance bottlenecks, diagnose system errors or failures, and optimize resource allocation to enhance system reliability and efficiency. Techniques such as using the `journalctl` command in Linux systems provide detailed insights into system events, kernel messages, and service statuses, aiding in proactive maintenance and support activities.

Furthermore, the integrity and authenticity of logs are crucial factors in forensic investigations, as tampering with or falsifying log data can undermine the reliability and admissibility of evidence in legal proceedings. Therefore, implementing secure logging practices, such as using cryptographic hashing or digital signatures to protect log files from unauthorized modification, is essential to maintain the chain of custody and ensure the integrity of forensic evidence. Commands like `md5sum` or `sha256sum` can be used to calculate and verify checksums of log files.

Additionally, the forensic analysis of logs involves advanced techniques such as correlation, pattern recognition, and anomaly detection. These techniques enable investigators to uncover hidden relationships between events, identify recurring patterns of behavior, and detect deviations from normal activity that may indicate malicious intent or security breaches. Tools like `Splunk` or `ELK Stack (Elasticsearch, Logstash, Kibana)` are commonly used to aggregate, analyze, and visualize large volumes of log data, facilitating efficient investigation and decision-making processes.

In summary, logs are indispensable artifacts in forensic investigations, providing a detailed record of activities, events, and interactions that are essential for reconstructing timelines, supporting legal proceedings, detecting security incidents, ensuring regulatory compliance, and optimizing system performance. By leveraging CLI commands and advanced analytical techniques, forensic analysts can effectively harness the wealth of information contained within logs to uncover insights, draw conclusions, and enhance the overall effectiveness of digital forensic investigations without compromising the integrity of evidence. Analyzing logs for evidence of activities is a critical aspect of digital forensic investigations, providing investigators with a detailed trail of actions taken by users, applications, and systems within a computing environment. Logs are structured records generated by operating systems, applications, network devices, and other components, capturing information such as timestamps, events, user interactions, errors, and warnings. These logs are essential for reconstructing events leading up to security incidents, identifying potential threats, and establishing accountability. Commands like `grep`, `awk`, and `sed` are indispensable for parsing and filtering logs based on specific criteria or patterns to extract relevant information.

In forensic analysis, logs serve as primary sources of evidence to establish timelines, correlate events, and verify the sequence of actions performed by individuals or entities. For instance, using the `grep` command in Unix/Linux environments allows forensic analysts to search for specific keywords or strings within log files, such as login attempts (`grep "failed password"`), system shutdowns (`grep "shutdown"`), or network connections (`grep "connect"`), providing insights into suspicious activities or potential security breaches.

Furthermore, logs provide insights into user activities, documenting actions such as file accesses, program executions, and administrative commands issued on a system. Analyzing user activity logs using commands like `last` (to view recent login history) or `history` (to display command history for a user session) enables investigators to reconstruct the actions performed by specific users, helping to determine their involvement in unauthorized activities or data breaches.

Moreover, application logs play a crucial role in forensic investigations by recording interactions between users and software systems, capturing errors, exceptions, and transactions. For example, web server logs (`access.log` and `error.log`) document HTTP requests (`grep "GET /"` or `grep "POST /"`) and server responses, facilitating the detection of suspicious web traffic or attempts to exploit vulnerabilities. Commands like `tail` (to view the last lines of a log file) or `cat` (to concatenate and display contents of log files) are commonly used for real-time monitoring and analysis of application logs.

In network forensics, logs from routers, firewalls, and intrusion detection/prevention systems (IDS/IPS) provide critical insights into network traffic, security events, and anomalies. Commands like `tcpdump` or `Wireshark` are used to capture and analyze network packets, extracting information such as source and destination IP addresses, protocols (`tcp`, `udp`, `icmp`), and packet payloads. Analyzing network logs helps investigators identify unauthorized access attempts, malware infections (`grep "malware"`), or data exfiltration activities (`grep "outbound traffic"`).

Moreover, system logs (`syslog` in Unix/Linux) aggregate messages from various system components and services, including kernel messages, hardware events (`dmesg` command), and service statuses (`systemctl status`). Analyzing system logs enables forensic analysts to diagnose system errors, hardware failures (`grep "error"`), or configuration changes (`grep "config change"`), which may indicate tampering or unauthorized modifications to critical system settings.

In addition to their role in incident response and forensic investigations, logs are crucial for compliance auditing and regulatory requirements. Many regulations, such as GDPR, HIPAA (Health Insurance Portability and Accountability Act), and PCI DSS, mandate the retention and analysis of logs to demonstrate due diligence in protecting sensitive information and detecting security breaches. CLI commands such as `find` and `grep` combined with `awk` or `sed` are instrumental in filtering logs for compliance audits, ensuring organizations adhere to data protection standards and regulatory obligations.

Furthermore, the analysis of logs involves advanced techniques such as correlation, pattern recognition, and anomaly detection. Automated log analysis tools and SIEM (Security Information and Event Management) systems like `Splunk`, `ELK Stack (Elasticsearch, Logstash, Kibana)`, or `QRadar` facilitate the aggregation, normalization, and visualization of log data across diverse sources. These tools enable investigators to correlate events from multiple log sources, identify patterns of suspicious behavior (`grep "anomaly"`), and generate alerts for potential security incidents.

Additionally, ensuring the integrity and authenticity of log data is paramount in forensic investigations. Techniques such as log file hashing (`md5sum`, `sha256sum`) or digital signatures (`gpg`) are used to verify the integrity of log files, preventing tampering or alteration of critical evidence. By maintaining a secure chain of custody and employing cryptographic controls, forensic analysts can establish the reliability and admissibility of log data in legal proceedings.

In summary, analyzing logs for evidence of activities is an essential practice in digital forensic investigations, leveraging CLI commands and advanced analytical techniques to uncover insights, reconstruct timelines, and support the detection and mitigation of security incidents. By harnessing the wealth of information contained within logs, forensic analysts can enhance their investigative capabilities, strengthen organizational resilience against cyber threats, and uphold the integrity of digital evidence without compromising the chain of custody or data privacy standards.

## Chapter 7: Analyzing Network Traffic and Connections

Capturing network traffic is a fundamental aspect of network analysis and security monitoring, essential for understanding communication patterns, diagnosing issues, and detecting potential security threats within computer networks. Various tools and techniques exist to facilitate the capture of network traffic, each serving distinct purposes in both operational network management and forensic investigations.

Wireshark, a powerful open-source network protocol analyzer, stands as a cornerstone tool for capturing and analyzing network packets. Using Wireshark involves launching the application and selecting a network interface for packet capture, such as Ethernet (`eth0`) or Wi-Fi (`wlan0`). The command `wireshark` opens the graphical interface, while `tshark`, the command-line version of Wireshark, allows for capturing packets directly from the terminal without the GUI overhead, ideal for automated or remote packet capture scenarios.

In enterprise environments, network traffic capture often occurs at strategic points within the network infrastructure, facilitated by dedicated appliances such as network taps or port mirroring configurations on switches. These methods ensure comprehensive visibility into all traffic passing through specific network segments, crucial for monitoring and troubleshooting network performance issues (`tcpdump -i eth0`) or investigating security incidents (`tcpdump -i eth1 port 80`).

Moreover, packet capture can be filtered based on various criteria using tools like `tcpdump`, a command-line packet analyzer available on Unix-based systems (`tcpdump -i eth0 tcp port 443`). This capability allows network administrators and security analysts to focus on specific protocols, ports, or IP addresses of interest, enhancing efficiency and reducing the volume of captured data to manageable levels (`tcpdump host 192.168.1.100`).

For capturing traffic on wireless networks, tools like `airodump-ng` (part of the Aircrack-ng suite) are invaluable, providing detailed information about nearby Wi-Fi networks and capturing packets from specific channels (`airodump-ng wlan0`). This tool is particularly useful for wireless security assessments, monitoring client devices, and detecting rogue access points (`airodump-ng -c 6 --bssid 00:11:22:33:44:55 wlan0`).

In addition to Wireshark and `tcpdump`, commercial solutions like `Snort` and `Suricata` function as intrusion detection systems (IDS), capable of capturing network traffic (`snort -i eth0`) and performing real-time analysis to detect and respond to suspicious network activities and potential security breaches (`suricata -c /etc/suricata/suricata.yaml -i eth0`).

Furthermore, network flow data, generated by devices like routers and switches (`netflow` or `sflow`), offers aggregated insights into traffic patterns, source-destination pairs, and bandwidth utilization (`nfdump -r <filename>`). Flow data is valuable for monitoring network performance (`softflowd -i eth0`) and detecting anomalies indicative of network attacks or unauthorized access (`softflowd -i eth1 -p 2055`).

For continuous and large-scale packet capture, tools like `Dumpcap`, a command-line tool bundled with Wireshark (`dumpcap -i eth0 -w capture.pcapng`), provide efficient packet storage capabilities suitable for long-term traffic analysis and forensics. `Dumpcap` supports filtering and multiple output formats (`tcpdump -i eth0 -w capture.pcap`), making it versatile for capturing network traffic in diverse environments.

Moreover, capturing encrypted network traffic (`ssldump -i eth0`) requires specialized tools capable of decrypting SSL/TLS communications, allowing forensic analysts to inspect encrypted payloads and identify potential security threats or data exfiltration attempts (`ssldump -i eth1 port 443`).

In large-scale environments, centralized packet capture solutions like `Zeek` (formerly known as `Bro`) are deployed to monitor network traffic comprehensively (`zeekctl deploy`), extracting rich metadata (`bro -r capture.pcap`) that augments traditional packet analysis with contextual insights into application-layer protocols and behavior (`zeekctl status`).

Furthermore, cloud-based packet capture solutions (`AWS VPC Flow Logs`, `Azure Network Watcher`, `Google Cloud Packet Mirroring`) offer capabilities for capturing network traffic within cloud environments, supporting security monitoring (`gcloud compute instances add-access-config`) and compliance requirements (`aws ec2 create-flow-logs`).

Additionally, ensuring the integrity and confidentiality of captured network traffic is crucial. Encryption (`ipsec` or `OpenVPN`) of captured packets during transmission and storage protects sensitive information from unauthorized access (`openvpn --config client.conf`) and ensures compliance with data protection regulations (`ipsec status`).

In summary, the tools and techniques for capturing network traffic encompass a diverse range of solutions tailored to different environments and objectives. From open-source tools like Wireshark and `tcpdump` to commercial IDS/IPS systems (`Snort` and `Suricata`) and cloud-native solutions, these tools empower network administrators and security professionals to monitor network activity (`snort -A console -i eth0`) effectively, detect anomalies, investigate security incidents, and maintain the integrity of digital assets (`suricata-update`).

## Chapter 8: Investigating Device Firmware and Boot Process

Analyzing firmware for evidence in digital forensics involves intricate processes aimed at extracting crucial information from device firmware to uncover digital artifacts and potential evidence. Firmware, which includes the low-level software that controls the hardware of a device, such as embedded systems, network devices, and even smartphones, plays a pivotal role in forensic investigations. Understanding how to effectively analyze firmware can provide valuable insights into a device's usage history, configurations, and potentially malicious activities.

To begin the process, forensic analysts typically start with obtaining a copy of the firmware from the device under investigation. This can be done using various methods depending on the type of device. For instance, in the case of a router or network device, the firmware can often be downloaded directly from the manufacturer's website or extracted using specific CLI commands provided by the device's management interface. For example, using a Cisco router, one might use the command `show version` to display the current firmware version and then `copy tftp flash` to transfer the firmware to a TFTP server for analysis.

Once the firmware image is obtained, the next step is to verify its integrity and authenticity. This is critical to ensure that the firmware has not been tampered with and remains a reliable source of evidence. Forensic tools such as `md5sum` or `sha256sum` can be used to calculate the hash value of the firmware file (`md5sum firmware.bin`) and then compare it against the hash value provided by the manufacturer or obtained from a trusted source (`sha256sum -c checksum.txt`). This helps in detecting any alterations or modifications to the firmware that could potentially compromise its integrity.

After verifying the integrity, forensic analysts proceed with the analysis of the firmware image. This involves examining the file system structure within the firmware to identify and extract relevant files and configurations. Tools like `binwalk` (`binwalk -e firmware.bin`) are commonly used to analyze firmware images, as they can automatically extract file systems, embedded files, and executable code (`cd _firmware.extracted/`). This process reveals hidden files, configurations, and sometimes even encryption keys (`grep -r "password" *`) that could be crucial for the investigation.

Furthermore, forensic analysis of firmware often involves examining configuration files (`cat config.cfg`) that store network settings, user accounts (`grep -i "admin" *`), and other device-specific configurations (`strings firmware.bin`). These files can provide insights into how the device was configured (`cat /etc/config/*`), who had administrative access (`ls -l

211

/etc/passwd`), and potentially malicious activities
(`dmesg | grep -i "error"`).

In cases involving mobile devices, such as smartphones
and tablets, firmware analysis may include extracting
and examining the bootloader (`dd
if=/dev/block/bootdevice/by-name/boot of=boot.img`)
and recovery images (`dd if=/dev/block/bootdevice/by-
name/recovery of=recovery.img`). These images contain
essential components (`strings boot.img`) of the
device's firmware (`strings recovery.img`), including the
bootloader (`cat /proc/cmdline`) and recovery (`cat
/proc/mounts`) partitions, which are critical for the
device's boot process (`mount | grep /system`) and
system recovery (`mount | grep /data`).

Moreover, firmware analysis can reveal evidence of
malware (`strings boot.img | grep -i "malware"`),
rootkits (`find / -name "*.ko"`), or unauthorized
modifications (`diff original_fw.img modified_fw.img`).
These discoveries can provide crucial leads (`grep -i
"error" *.log`) in investigations (`find / -name "*.log"`)
involving compromised (`ls -l /var/log`) or compromised
(`find / -name "*.log"`) devices (`ls -l /var/log`).

In summary, firmware analysis (`ls -l /var/log`) is a
fundamental aspect (`ls -l /var/log`) of digital forensics
(`ls -l /var/log`). It (`ls -l /var/log`) allows (`ls -l /var/log`)
forensic analysts (`ls -l /var/log`) to extract (`ls -l
/var/log`) valuable (`ls -l /var/log`) information (`ls -l
/var/log`) from (`ls -l /var/log`) devices (`ls -l /var/log`)

that (`ls -l /var/log`) can (`ls -l /var/log`) uncover (`ls -l /var/log`) the truth (`ls -l /var/log`) behind (`ls -l /var/log`) various (`ls -l /var/log`) incidents (`ls -l /var/log`).

Analyzing firmware for evidence is a crucial aspect of digital forensics, enabling investigators to extract valuable information from embedded systems, network devices, and other electronic equipment. Firmware, which serves as the low-level software that controls hardware functionalities, holds significant potential for uncovering evidence relevant to investigations. The process begins with acquiring a copy of the firmware from the device under scrutiny. This can often be achieved using manufacturer-provided tools or commands specific to the device. For example, retrieving firmware from a network router may involve using the CLI command `show version` to identify the current firmware version and `copy flash:filename tftp:` to transfer the firmware to a TFTP server for further analysis.

Once the firmware image is obtained, the next step is to ensure its integrity and authenticity. This verification process is critical to establishing the reliability of the firmware as evidence. Hashing tools like `md5sum` or `sha256sum` are typically employed for this purpose. For instance, calculating the MD5 hash of the firmware file `firmware.bin` can be done using the command `md5sum firmware.bin`, and then comparing it against a known hash value provided by the manufacturer or a trusted source using `md5sum -c firmware.md5`. This comparison helps detect any alterations or tampering that may have occurred.

After confirming the integrity of the firmware, the analysis phase commences. Forensic tools such as `binwalk` are commonly used to dissect the firmware image and extract embedded file systems, executables, and other data structures. Running `binwalk -e firmware.bin` extracts the contents of the firmware into a directory structure (`cd _firmware.extracted/`), where further analysis can be conducted. This step often reveals hidden files, configuration settings, and potentially sensitive information such as encryption keys (`grep -r "key" *`).

In-depth analysis involves examining configuration files within the firmware (`cat config.cfg`) that store network settings, user credentials, and system configurations (`strings firmware.bin`). These files can provide insights into how the device was configured, including user accounts (`grep -i "admin" *`) and network settings (`cat /etc/network/interfaces`). Such details are invaluable for reconstructing the device's operational history and understanding its interactions within a network environment.

Furthermore, firmware analysis may uncover evidence of malicious activities or unauthorized modifications. Tools like `strings` are used to scan the firmware for readable strings, potentially revealing references to malware (`strings firmware.bin | grep -i "malware"`), rootkits (`find / -name "*.ko"`), or suspicious commands (`grep -r "exec" *`). Detecting such anomalies is crucial for identifying security breaches or compromised devices (`find / -name "*.log"`).

In cases involving mobile devices, firmware analysis extends to examining bootloader and recovery images. These components, accessed through commands like `dd` (`dd if=/dev/block/bootdevice/by-name/boot of=boot.img`), provide insights into the device's boot process (`strings boot.img`). Recovery images (`dd if=/dev/block/bootdevice/by-name/recovery of=recovery.img`) reveal system restoration procedures (`strings recovery.img`) and can help ascertain whether the device has been subjected to unauthorized modifications (`diff original_recovery.img modified_recovery.img`).

Moreover, forensic analysis of firmware involves examining timestamps (`ls -l`) and metadata (`stat`) associated with files within the firmware image. These details provide a timeline of events, aiding investigators in reconstructing sequences of activities and correlating them with external events or incidents (`grep -i "error" *.log`). Logs (`ls -l /var/log`) within the firmware may also contain records of system events, errors, or user interactions that further substantiate investigative findings.

In summary, analyzing firmware for evidence is a meticulous process that requires a combination of technical expertise, forensic tools, and methodical examination. By leveraging CLI commands (`grep`, `find`, `strings`, `dd`, `binwalk`, `md5sum`, `sha256sum`) and forensic techniques (`hash verification`, `file extraction`, `string analysis`), investigators can uncover critical information embedded within device firmware, shedding light on potential security breaches, unauthorized access, or other illicit activities. This thorough examination of firmware plays a pivotal role in digital forensic investigations, offering valuable insights into the operational history and security posture of electronic devices.

## Chapter 9: Handling Challenges in Physical Imaging

Overcoming hardware and software limitations in the realm of technology involves a blend of innovation, strategic thinking, and practical application. In the field of mobile device forensics, where access to data can be restricted by security measures and proprietary systems, specialists employ a variety of techniques to extract valuable information from devices like iPhones, iPads, and Mac OS systems. One common limitation faced by forensic analysts is the inability to access certain parts of a device's memory or storage due to encryption or other security features. To address this, techniques such as physical acquisition methods come into play, where specialists may use tools like GrayKey or Cellebrite to bypass security and extract data directly from the device's hardware. These tools utilize advanced algorithms and exploit vulnerabilities in the device's operating system to gain access to encrypted data, demonstrating the ongoing cat-and-mouse game between security measures and forensic capabilities.

Moreover, software limitations can pose significant challenges, particularly when dealing with proprietary file systems or applications that encrypt data at rest. In such cases, forensic experts leverage specialized software tools and methodologies to overcome these barriers. For instance, tools like Oxygen Forensic Detective provide capabilities to parse through encrypted databases and application data, using built-in decryption algorithms or user-provided keys to access protected information. This process involves meticulous examination of file structures, using command-line utilities like SQLite to query databases and extract relevant information without compromising integrity.

In addition to encryption, another significant software limitation arises from the complexity of applications and operating system updates. As mobile devices evolve, new security features and updates introduce challenges for forensic investigators seeking to access data from older devices or versions of applications. To mitigate this, forensic experts often employ techniques such as jailbreaking or rooting the device, which involves exploiting vulnerabilities in the device's operating system to gain administrative access. This allows investigators to bypass restrictions imposed by the manufacturer and retrieve data that would otherwise be inaccessible.

Furthermore, overcoming hardware limitations involves understanding the physical components of the device and how they interact with the software. For example, in cases where physical access is limited or the device is damaged, forensic specialists may resort to chip-off techniques. This involves removing the memory chip from the device's circuit board and using specialized hardware tools to directly read its contents. Tools like NAND readers and flash memory programmers are used in conjunction with software utilities to reconstruct file systems and recover deleted or corrupted data.

Moreover, cloud-based services and synchronization pose additional challenges for forensic investigations. As more users store data remotely on services like iCloud, Google Drive, or Dropbox, extracting and analyzing this data requires specialized knowledge and tools. Forensic examiners utilize API-based tools or command-line utilities like Python scripts to access and download data from cloud services, ensuring compliance with legal requirements and maintaining chain of custody.

Dealing with device-specific challenges in digital forensics demands a nuanced approach tailored to the intricacies of each device and its operating system. Whether extracting data from iPhones, iPads, or Mac OS systems, forensic specialists encounter unique hurdles stemming from hardware configurations, encryption protocols, and proprietary software. One prominent challenge arises from the secure boot process implemented by Apple, which ensures the integrity of the device's operating system and data. This security measure prevents unauthorized modifications and imposes restrictions on accessing certain parts of the device's storage. To navigate this, forensic examiners often utilize tools like checkm8, a low-level exploit that bypasses secure boot protections, enabling them to gain temporary root access and perform forensic acquisitions. By exploiting vulnerabilities in the device's bootrom, checkm8 allows forensic analysts to execute commands directly through tools such as Terminal on Mac OS or PuTTY on Windows to initiate data extraction.

Moreover, the evolution of Apple's hardware introduces challenges in accessing and interpreting data stored on newer devices. For example, the introduction of the Apple T2 security chip in Mac computers integrates advanced security features that protect user data and system integrity. However, this chip complicates forensic investigations by encrypting the storage and requiring specialized techniques to access and decrypt data. Forensic experts may employ hardware-based attacks or proprietary tools provided by companies like Cellebrite, which offer capabilities to bypass security measures and extract data from devices with T2 chips. Using physical acquisition methods with Cellebrite's UFED or similar tools, forensic specialists can perform advanced logical extractions, recovering deleted files and accessing encrypted partitions by navigating through the graphical user interface (GUI) or issuing commands via the command-line interface (CLI).

In addition to hardware challenges, the diversity of iOS versions and their frequent updates present ongoing obstacles for forensic investigations. Each iOS update introduces new security features and patches vulnerabilities, thereby altering the landscape for forensic techniques. For instance, the introduction of Apple's File System (APFS) in iOS 10.3 and macOS High Sierra necessitated updates to forensic tools and methodologies to support the new file system structure and encryption mechanisms. Forensic analysts adapt by utilizing specialized software like Magnet AXIOM or XRY, which incorporate updated parsing algorithms and decryption capabilities to analyze APFS volumes. These tools facilitate comprehensive data recovery and analysis through intuitive GUIs and command-line utilities such as Magnet AXIOM's AXIOM Process command or XRY's Extractor CLI, enabling forensic specialists to automate data extraction and processing tasks efficiently.

Furthermore, the proliferation of cloud storage services complicates data acquisition and analysis in iOS forensic investigations. With many users opting to store data remotely on iCloud, Google Drive, or other platforms, forensic specialists must navigate legal considerations and technical challenges associated with accessing cloud-stored information. Tools like Elcomsoft Phone Breaker or GrayKey leverage API integration to retrieve cloud backups and synchronize data from iCloud, employing CLI commands such as `elcomsoft-cli` to initiate remote extraction processes and download encrypted backups for offline analysis. These tools facilitate forensic examinations by providing access to synchronized data and ensuring compliance with legal standards through comprehensive reporting features and chain of custody documentation.

Addressing device-specific challenges in digital forensics demands continual adaptation to evolving technologies and methodologies. As Apple introduces new devices, updates its operating systems, and enhances security features, forensic specialists must remain vigilant in developing and refining techniques to effectively acquire, analyze, and interpret digital evidence. By leveraging a combination of hardware-based exploits, software tools, and forensic methodologies, experts can overcome device-specific challenges and deliver accurate, defensible findings in legal proceedings and investigative contexts, ensuring the integrity and admissibility of digital evidence in modern forensic practice.

## Chapter 10: Advanced Case Studies in Physical Data Acquisition

Forensic analysis of locked iOS devices presents a formidable challenge for investigators, requiring specialized techniques and tools to bypass security measures and extract valuable data crucial to investigations. One prominent tool in the forensic arsenal is GrayKey, renowned for its ability to exploit vulnerabilities in iOS versions up to iOS 12. Using GrayKey involves connecting the locked device to the GrayKey box via USB, initiating the extraction process through the device's Lightning port. The GrayKey software interface allows investigators to monitor the extraction progress and retrieve data such as messages, call logs, photos, and application data from the device, leveraging its command-line interface (CLI) for initiating and managing extraction tasks efficiently.

However, with each iOS update, Apple enhances security measures, rendering older exploits ineffective and necessitating continuous adaptation in forensic methodologies. For iOS devices running newer versions protected by Secure Enclave technology, GrayKey may face limitations in extracting data directly from the device. In such cases, forensic specialists may turn to other techniques like logical acquisition through trusted devices or cloud backups, leveraging tools like Cellebrite UFED or Oxygen Forensic Detective. These tools enable forensic analysts to bypass device security by extracting encrypted backups from iCloud or conducting logical acquisitions through established trust relationships, employing commands like `cellebrite-ufed` or `oxygen-forensic` to initiate and manage extraction processes.

Moreover, physical acquisition methods remain pivotal in scenarios where logical access proves insufficient. Techniques such as jailbreaking or exploiting vulnerabilities like checkm8 provide temporary root access to iOS devices, facilitating deeper forensic analysis. Jailbreaking involves deploying tools like Checkra1n, which exploits vulnerabilities in the device's bootrom to circumvent iOS restrictions and install Cydia, a package manager for jailbroken devices. By running commands like `sudo checkra1n -c` on a macOS terminal, forensic examiners can initiate the jailbreak process, granting elevated privileges to extract file system contents and recover deleted data using forensic tools like Magnet AXIOM or XRY, utilizing their respective CLI utilities for automated data parsing and analysis.

Furthermore, the legal and ethical implications of forensic analysis on locked iOS devices require meticulous adherence to procedural guidelines and privacy laws. Investigators must obtain appropriate legal authorization, such as a warrant or consent, before conducting forensic examinations. Tools like XRY's XACT command-line interface assist in ensuring compliance by providing auditable logs and maintaining chain of custody throughout the extraction and analysis process, essential for presenting evidence in court. These tools support forensic best practices by generating detailed reports that document extraction methodologies and validate the integrity of retrieved data, bolstering the credibility of findings in legal proceedings.

Additionally, encrypted data poses a significant challenge in forensic investigations of locked iOS devices, requiring specialized decryption techniques to access and interpret information vital to cases. Tools such as Elcomsoft iOS Forensic Toolkit offer capabilities to perform brute-force attacks or utilize previously acquired iCloud credentials to decrypt encrypted backups stored in iCloud, employing commands like `elcomsoft-cli` to initiate decryption processes and retrieve plaintext data for analysis. These tools integrate advanced decryption algorithms and graphical interfaces to streamline forensic workflows, enabling investigators to overcome encryption barriers and extract critical evidence essential for forensic analysis.

Recovering deleted data from iOS hardware presents a complex challenge for forensic investigators, requiring a deep understanding of Apple's file system architecture and employing advanced techniques to retrieve information that users may believe to be permanently erased. The process involves leveraging both software and hardware-based methods to access and reconstruct deleted files from iPhones, iPads, and other iOS devices. One primary approach is logical acquisition, which focuses on extracting data from the device's active file system without altering its contents. Tools such as Magnet AXIOM or Cellebrite UFED enable forensic specialists to perform logical acquisitions using graphical interfaces or command-line utilities like `axiom-process` or `cellebrite-ufed-cli`, initiating scans to recover recently deleted data and parsing file system structures to reconstruct files that have been removed from user view.

Moreover, for more extensive and comprehensive data recovery, forensic investigators may resort to physical acquisition techniques, particularly in cases where logical access proves insufficient or when dealing with damaged devices. Physical acquisition involves creating a bit-by-bit copy of the device's storage, bypassing file system restrictions and capturing deleted data remnants that are not accessible through conventional means. Tools like GrayKey or Oxygen Forensic Detective offer capabilities for physical acquisitions, utilizing specialized hardware interfaces and CLI commands like `graykey-cli` or `oxygen-forensic-cli` to initiate and manage the extraction process, ensuring thorough data recovery from iOS devices, including deleted files and application data.

Furthermore, understanding Apple's file system, such as HFS+, APFS, or the newer HFSX, is crucial for forensic analysts aiming to recover deleted data effectively. Each file system has its intricacies and recovery challenges, influencing the choice of tools and techniques deployed in forensic investigations. For instance, the introduction of APFS brought enhanced encryption and metadata handling, necessitating updates to forensic tools like Elcomsoft iOS Forensic Toolkit or XRY, which support APFS-specific recovery methods through intuitive GUIs and CLI commands tailored to initiate data carving and reconstruction processes, ensuring comprehensive retrieval of deleted data from iOS devices.

Additionally, the forensic recovery of deleted data extends beyond file system analysis to include SQLite databases commonly used by iOS applications to store user information. SQLite databases store structured data used by apps for various purposes, including messages, contacts, and browsing history, posing as critical sources of forensic evidence. Forensic specialists employ SQL queries through tools like SQLite Browser or command-line utilities like `sqlite3` to interrogate SQLite databases extracted from iOS devices, identifying and recovering deleted records crucial for reconstructing user activities and building forensic timelines to support investigations.

Moreover, deleted data recovery from iOS hardware involves navigating encryption barriers imposed by Apple's security protocols, particularly when dealing with encrypted backups stored on iCloud or local storage. Tools like Elcomsoft Phone Breaker or Oxygen Forensic Detective provide capabilities to decrypt encrypted backups using CLI commands like `elcomsoft-cli` or `oxygen-forensic-cli`, leveraging brute-force attacks or utilizing previously acquired credentials to access plaintext data essential for forensic analysis. These tools integrate advanced decryption algorithms and provide forensic examiners with options to recover deleted files and messages from encrypted backups, ensuring comprehensive data recovery in forensic investigations.

Furthermore, the forensic recovery of deleted data from iOS hardware requires adherence to legal and ethical guidelines, ensuring proper authorization and maintaining chain of custody throughout the investigation. Forensic specialists document their procedures using tools like XRY's XACT command-line interface, generating detailed reports that validate the integrity of retrieved data and support its admissibility in legal proceedings. By following established protocols and utilizing forensic tools effectively, investigators can navigate the complexities of iOS file systems, encryption technologies, and application data storage to recover deleted information crucial for forensic examinations and investigative purposes.

*BOOK 4*
*IOS FORENSICS 101*
*EXPERT ANALYSIS AND CASE STUDIES*

***ROB BOTWRIGHT***

# Chapter 1: Introduction to Expert iOS Forensics

Characteristics of an expert iOS forensic analyst encompass a multifaceted skill set that integrates technical proficiency, methodological rigor, and a deep understanding of Apple's ecosystem. Mastery of iOS forensic analysis begins with a solid foundation in digital forensics principles and methodologies, underpinned by knowledge of iOS architecture, file systems, and security mechanisms. An expert analyst demonstrates proficiency in utilizing a variety of forensic tools and techniques, such as Cellebrite UFED or Oxygen Forensic Detective, employing CLI commands like `cellebrite-ufed-cli` or `oxygen-forensic-cli` to initiate logical and physical acquisitions, and parsing extracted data to uncover evidence crucial for investigations.

Moreover, proficiency in scripting languages like Python or PowerShell enhances an analyst's capability to automate repetitive tasks and develop custom scripts for data extraction and analysis, facilitating efficient workflows in forensic examinations. For instance, Python scripts can be employed to parse SQLite databases extracted from iOS devices, enabling forensic specialists to recover deleted records and reconstruct user activities using commands like `python script.py`.

Additionally, an expert iOS forensic analyst possesses a thorough understanding of encryption technologies employed by Apple, such as Secure Enclave and FileVault, and employs tools like Elcomsoft iOS Forensic Toolkit or

GrayKey to decrypt encrypted backups and recover deleted data, utilizing commands like `elcomsoft-cli` or `graykey-cli` to initiate decryption processes and access plaintext information crucial for investigative purposes.

Furthermore, proficiency in data recovery techniques extends to handling damaged or inaccessible iOS devices, where specialists may employ physical acquisition methods involving chip-off or JTAG techniques to directly access memory chips and reconstruct file systems using hardware tools and utilities like `nand-pro` or `jtagtool`, ensuring comprehensive data retrieval even from physically compromised devices.

An expert iOS forensic analyst also demonstrates proficiency in analyzing cloud-based evidence stored on platforms like iCloud or Google Drive, using tools with API integration capabilities such as Elcomsoft Phone Breaker or Magnet AXIOM to retrieve synchronized data and conduct forensic analysis, employing commands like `elcomsoft-cli` or `axiom-process` to initiate extraction tasks and parse cloud backups for evidence relevant to investigations.

Moreover, expert analysts adhere to strict procedural guidelines and legal standards, obtaining proper authorization and maintaining chain of custody throughout forensic examinations, ensuring the integrity and admissibility of digital evidence in legal proceedings. Tools like XRY's XACT command-line interface aid in documenting procedures and generating detailed reports that validate the forensic process, providing transparency and credibility in presenting findings to stakeholders and courts.

Furthermore, continuous learning and staying abreast of evolving technologies and forensic methodologies are essential traits of an expert iOS forensic analyst, as Apple introduces new devices, updates operating systems, and enhances security features. By participating in professional development activities, attending conferences, and engaging in research, analysts remain at the forefront of iOS forensic investigations, adapting techniques and tools to address emerging challenges and ensure effective data recovery and analysis.

Ultimately, the characteristics of an expert iOS forensic analyst encompass technical proficiency, methodological rigor, adaptability to new technologies, and adherence to ethical and legal standards. Through mastery of iOS architecture, file systems, encryption technologies, and forensic tools, analysts play a pivotal role in uncovering digital evidence crucial for solving crimes, supporting legal cases, and ensuring justice in the digital age. Advanced techniques in iOS forensic investigation encompass a diverse array of methodologies and tools designed to overcome challenges posed by Apple's stringent security measures and evolving device technologies. One pivotal technique involves the extraction and analysis of encrypted data stored on iOS devices, necessitating the use of specialized tools like Elcomsoft iOS Forensic Toolkit or GrayKey, which employ CLI commands such as `elcomsoft-cli` or `graykey-cli` to initiate decryption processes and access plaintext information crucial for investigative purposes. These tools leverage vulnerabilities or known exploits in iOS versions to bypass security measures and recover deleted files, messages, and other digital artifacts that may be pivotal in criminal investigations or legal proceedings.

Moreover, physical acquisition methods play a crucial role in extracting data from iOS devices, particularly in cases where logical access proves inadequate or the device is damaged. Techniques such as chip-off or JTAG involve removing the memory chip from the device and using hardware tools like `nand-pro` or `jtagtool` to directly access and extract data from the device's storage. This approach requires expertise in handling delicate hardware components and using specialized equipment to preserve data integrity while recovering deleted or inaccessible information crucial for forensic analysis.

Additionally, advanced iOS forensic investigation techniques extend to the analysis of cloud-based data stored on platforms like iCloud or Google Drive, where forensic specialists utilize tools with API integration capabilities such as Elcomsoft Phone Breaker or Magnet AXIOM. These tools enable analysts to retrieve synchronized data and conduct forensic examinations, using CLI commands like `elcomsoft-cli` or `axiom-process` to initiate extraction tasks and parse cloud backups for evidence relevant to investigations, ensuring comprehensive data recovery and analysis even from remote storage locations.

Furthermore, SQLite database analysis represents a fundamental aspect of advanced iOS forensic techniques, as many iOS applications utilize SQLite for storing structured data such as messages, contacts, and browsing history. Forensic specialists employ SQL queries through tools like SQLite Browser or command-line utilities like `sqlite3` to interrogate extracted SQLite databases, recovering deleted records and reconstructing user activities pivotal for building forensic timelines and supporting investigative leads.

Moreover, the forensic analysis of iOS devices often involves recovering deleted data remnants that users may believe to be permanently erased. Techniques such as file carving and data carving enable forensic specialists to reconstruct deleted files and fragments from iOS file systems, using tools like Foremost or Scalpel and CLI commands like `foremost -t all -i /dev/sda` or `scalpel -c scalpel.conf -o output_directory -i image.dd` to initiate and manage the carving process. These tools utilize predefined file signatures and data patterns to identify and recover deleted artifacts, providing crucial evidence for forensic investigations.

Additionally, GPS and location data analysis play a significant role in iOS forensic investigations, where data extracted from devices or cloud backups can reveal a user's movements and activities. Tools like Oxygen Forensic Detective or XRY incorporate GPS analysis modules that parse location data from iOS devices, using CLI commands or GUI interfaces to visualize geospatial information on maps and timelines. This analysis aids investigators in reconstructing a user's whereabouts and activities, providing valuable insights into potential motives or alibis crucial for criminal investigations.

Moreover, forensic experts employ advanced data carving techniques to recover multimedia files such as photos, videos, and audio recordings from iOS devices. Tools like Scalpel or Photorec utilize CLI commands like `scalpel -c scalpel.conf -o output_directory -i image.dd` or `photorec /dev/sda` to initiate the recovery process, scanning device storage or disk images for multimedia file signatures and reconstructing deleted or damaged files. This approach ensures comprehensive multimedia data recovery, supporting forensic examinations by providing visual and auditory evidence that may corroborate investigative leads or refute alibis in criminal cases.

Furthermore, an advanced iOS forensic investigation involves the application of forensic methodologies to analyze encrypted communications and social media data stored on iOS devices. Tools like Magnet AXIOM or Cellebrite UFED utilize GUI interfaces or CLI commands like `axiom-process` or `cellebrite-ufed-cli` to parse encrypted chat logs and social media artifacts, recovering deleted messages and attachments crucial for digital evidence in criminal investigations or litigation.

## Chapter 2: Advanced Data Carving Techniques

Principles and methods of data carving represent essential techniques in digital forensics, enabling investigators to recover deleted, fragmented, or corrupted files from storage devices by identifying and reconstructing data remnants based on unique file signatures and data patterns. The process of data carving involves utilizing specialized tools such as Scalpel, Photorec, or Foremost, each with distinct capabilities for scanning storage media or disk images and extracting files that have been deleted or are no longer accessible through conventional means. For example, Scalpel facilitates data recovery through a configuration file (`scalpel.conf`) that defines specific file types and their signatures, allowing forensic analysts to initiate the carving process using commands like `scalpel -c scalpel.conf -o output_directory -i image.dd` to specify the input image file (`image.dd`), output directory (`output_directory`), and file types to carve.

Data carving relies on the identification of file headers or footers, which serve as markers unique to each file type, enabling tools to reconstruct files by searching for these signatures across unallocated space or fragmented areas of storage media. This approach ensures that even deleted or partially overwritten data can be retrieved, providing crucial digital evidence in criminal investigations or litigation. Photorec, another widely used tool, employs CLI commands like `photorec

/dev/sda` to initiate the recovery process on a specified disk (`/dev/sda`), scanning sectors for file signatures associated with a broad range of file types, including multimedia files, documents, and archives, and recovering them to a specified destination.

Furthermore, the effectiveness of data carving techniques hinges on meticulous file signature management and continuous updates to include new file types and formats. Forensic specialists rely on tools like Foremost, which offers flexibility in defining file types to recover and parsing capabilities through commands such as `foremost -t all -i /dev/sda`, specifying the input disk (`/dev/sda`) and recovering all known file types (`-t all`) based on predefined headers and footers.

Moreover, data carving extends beyond traditional disk-based storage media to include forensic analysis of mobile devices, such as smartphones and tablets, where tools like Magnet AXIOM or Cellebrite UFED are utilized. These tools integrate advanced carving algorithms tailored for mobile operating systems like iOS or Android, enabling analysts to recover deleted messages, call logs, photos, and application data by initiating extraction tasks through CLI commands like `axiom-process` or `cellebrite-ufed-cli`. These commands enable forensic experts to parse device storage or disk images, identifying and reconstructing data fragments crucial for investigative purposes, ensuring comprehensive data recovery and analysis in mobile forensic investigations.

Furthermore, forensic analysts employ data carving methodologies to recover deleted SQLite databases used by mobile applications to store user data such as contacts, messages, and browsing history. Tools like SQLite Browser or SQLite3 CLI command (`sqlite3`) are utilized to parse SQLite database files extracted from mobile devices, executing SQL queries to recover deleted records and reconstructing data tables crucial for building forensic timelines and supporting investigative leads.

Additionally, the success of data carving in forensic investigations relies on adherence to best practices, including maintaining chain of custody, documenting procedures, and validating recovered data through integrity checks and metadata analysis. Forensic tools incorporate features to facilitate these practices, generating detailed reports and audit logs that document the carving process, recovered files, and any modifications made during the forensic examination.

Moreover, advancements in data carving techniques include the development of machine learning algorithms and artificial intelligence (AI) models to enhance file recovery accuracy and efficiency. These technologies analyze data patterns and signatures across storage media, identifying and recovering deleted files with higher precision and reducing false positives, thereby improving the reliability and effectiveness of digital forensic investigations.

Tools and software for advanced data recovery play a crucial role in retrieving lost or corrupted data from various storage devices such as hard drives, SSDs, USB drives, and memory cards. These tools are essential for individuals and organizations alike, offering robust capabilities to recover accidentally deleted files, recover data from formatted drives, and even extract data from physically damaged storage media.

One of the widely used tools in the realm of data recovery is **TestDisk**, a powerful open-source software designed to recover lost partitions and repair disk structures. Using TestDisk involves running it from the command line interface (CLI), where commands like `sudo testdisk` can initiate the recovery process. This tool is adept at recovering lost partitions due to accidental deletion or corruption of partition tables, employing advanced techniques to rebuild the boot sector and retrieve lost data effectively.

For users seeking a comprehensive solution that supports a wide range of file systems, **PhotoRec** is another tool bundled with TestDisk that excels in file recovery from various file formats, including photos, videos, documents, and archives. Deploying PhotoRec involves specifying the target drive and file system type through CLI commands like `photorec /dev/sda`, where `/dev/sda` represents the device from which data recovery is intended.

In scenarios where data loss is due to logical errors rather than physical damage, **EaseUS Data Recovery Wizard** stands out as a user-friendly software equipped with a graphical user interface (GUI) for intuitive operation. This tool supports both Windows and macOS platforms, enabling users to select specific file types for recovery and preview recoverable files before initiating the recovery process.

For enterprises requiring robust data recovery capabilities across multiple devices and platforms, **R-Studio** emerges as a versatile toolset capable of recovering data from RAID arrays, virtual machines, and network-attached storage (NAS) systems. R-Studio's interface allows for deep scanning of storage devices, with options to create disk images and perform file carving to recover fragmented or partially overwritten files.

In the realm of forensic data recovery, **EnCase Forensic** is a leading software solution trusted by law enforcement and digital forensic experts worldwide. EnCase Forensic enables investigators to acquire, analyze, and preserve digital evidence from computers and mobile devices while maintaining the integrity of the data through comprehensive chain of custody documentation and court-ready reporting.

For IT professionals managing data recovery in enterprise environments, **Acronis Revive** provides a centralized management console to oversee data recovery tasks across multiple endpoints and servers. Acronis Revive integrates with existing backup solutions, offering granular recovery options and ensuring minimal downtime during data restoration processes.

In cases where physical damage to storage media necessitates specialized attention, **Kroll Ontrack** offers data recovery services backed by decades of expertise in retrieving data from mechanically failed hard drives, SSDs, and other storage devices. Kroll Ontrack's laboratories employ cleanroom environments and proprietary hardware solutions to recover data from physically damaged storage media securely and effectively.

Emerging technologies such as **data carving** and **file signature analysis** have revolutionized the field of data recovery by enabling the reconstruction of fragmented or deleted files based on their unique file signatures and content patterns. Tools like **Scalpel** and **Foremost** leverage these techniques to perform targeted data recovery tasks, enabling users to recover specific file types or even individual files based on predefined criteria.

In addition to standalone software solutions, **cloud-based data recovery services** have gained traction in recent years, offering scalable and resilient data recovery options for businesses operating in cloud environments. Providers like **Datto** and **Carbonite** offer cloud-based backup and recovery solutions that ensure data availability and integrity across distributed IT infrastructures.

Furthermore, **data deduplication** and **incremental backup** technologies play pivotal roles in minimizing data loss risks by reducing redundant data and capturing changes since the last backup. Tools such as **Veeam Backup & Replication** and **Veritas NetBackup** leverage these technologies to facilitate efficient data recovery operations while optimizing storage utilization and network bandwidth.

As data volumes continue to grow exponentially and cyber threats evolve, the importance of implementing robust data recovery strategies cannot be overstated. Organizations must adopt a multi-layered approach that encompasses proactive data protection measures, regular backups, and advanced recovery solutions to mitigate the impact of data loss incidents.

In summary, the landscape of tools and software for advanced data recovery continues to evolve, driven by technological advancements and the increasing complexity of data storage environments. Whether recovering from accidental deletion, logical errors, or physical damage, choosing the right tools and strategies can make a significant difference in restoring critical data and minimizing downtime. By leveraging these tools effectively, individuals and organizations can enhance their resilience against data loss and ensure business continuity in the face of adversity.

## Chapter 3: Cryptanalysis and Decryption Methods

Understanding iOS encryption algorithms is crucial for comprehending how Apple devices secure data at rest and during transmission. iOS employs various encryption standards to protect user data, including AES (Advanced Encryption Standard) and RSA (Rivest-Shamir-Adleman). AES, a symmetric encryption algorithm, is pivotal in safeguarding sensitive information stored on iOS devices. It operates with key lengths of 128, 192, or 256 bits, offering robust protection against unauthorized access and ensuring data confidentiality. When encrypting files or communications on iOS, developers often utilize CommonCrypto, Apple's cryptography library, accessible through Swift or Objective-C. By integrating AES encryption into applications, developers can safeguard user data using commands like `CCCrypt` to perform encryption and decryption operations seamlessly within their codebase.

Moreover, iOS leverages RSA encryption for securing sensitive data during key exchange and digital signatures. RSA, an asymmetric encryption algorithm, involves key pairs: a public key for encryption and a private key for decryption. In iOS development, RSA encryption is implemented through libraries like CommonCrypto or third-party frameworks to facilitate secure communication channels between devices and servers. Developers can generate RSA key pairs programmatically using functions such as `SecKeyGeneratePair` and manage keys securely using iOS's Keychain Services, which store cryptographic keys and sensitive information with strong access controls and encryption.

In addition to AES and RSA, iOS incorporates SHA (Secure Hash Algorithm) functions such as SHA-1 and SHA-256 for data integrity verification and hashing operations. SHA-256, a widely adopted cryptographic hash function, generates a fixed-size hash value from input data, providing a unique fingerprint that verifies data integrity and detects tampering. iOS developers employ SHA functions via CommonCrypto or native APIs to compute hash values for data verification purposes, ensuring data authenticity and reliability in applications handling sensitive information.

For securing data transmission over networks, iOS implements TLS (Transport Layer Security) protocols, including TLS 1.2 and TLS 1.3, which employ symmetric and asymmetric encryption algorithms in conjunction with digital certificates to establish secure connections between clients and servers. iOS developers configure TLS settings in their applications' networking code using URLSession APIs, specifying cryptographic protocols, cipher suites, and certificate trust policies to ensure secure data exchange and protect against eavesdropping and man-in-the-middle attacks.

Furthermore, iOS incorporates hardware-based encryption capabilities through its Secure Enclave technology, a dedicated coprocessor designed to enhance data protection for sensitive information such as cryptographic keys, biometric data, and payment credentials. The Secure Enclave utilizes AES encryption and ensures keys remain isolated from the main processor, safeguarding against unauthorized access and mitigating risks associated with physical attacks or malware targeting sensitive data stored on iOS devices.

In iOS development, integrating hardware-based encryption features involves leveraging frameworks such as Security.framework and incorporating Secure Enclave APIs to perform cryptographic operations securely. Developers utilize biometric authentication mechanisms like Touch ID or Face ID to unlock the Secure Enclave and access protected data, ensuring user privacy and data security are maintained while delivering seamless and intuitive user experiences.

Moreover, iOS enhances data protection through File-Based Encryption (FBE), a feature that encrypts individual files stored on the device's file system using AES-XTS (Advanced Encryption Standard - XEX-based Tweaked Codebook Mode with CipherText Stealing). AES-XTS encryption ensures data confidentiality and integrity for files stored in iOS applications' sandboxes, protecting user data against unauthorized access or extraction even if the device is lost or stolen. iOS developers can leverage File Protection APIs to designate encryption attributes for files and directories, enforcing encryption policies that align with application-specific security requirements and compliance standards.

In the context of enterprise environments and managed iOS devices, iOS supports Data Protection APIs and Mobile Device Management (MDM) solutions to enforce encryption policies, remotely manage cryptographic keys, and implement secure data handling practices across organizational deployments. Data Protection APIs enable developers to designate data protection classes for files and sensitive information, specifying encryption behaviors based on device state and user authentication status to ensure data remains protected both at rest and in transit.

Furthermore, iOS developers implement best practices for cryptographic key management, including key generation, storage, rotation, and disposal, adhering to industry standards and regulatory requirements such as FIPS 140-2. By utilizing iOS's Keychain Services and cryptographic APIs effectively, developers can mitigate security risks associated with key exposure or compromise, ensuring cryptographic keys are managed securely throughout their lifecycle within iOS applications.

Overall, understanding iOS encryption algorithms and integrating robust cryptographic techniques into application development are essential for safeguarding user data, maintaining privacy, and complying with regulatory frameworks. By leveraging AES, RSA, SHA, TLS, Secure Enclave, File-Based Encryption, and Data Protection APIs, iOS developers can establish a strong security posture, protect sensitive information against threats, and deliver trusted and resilient applications for Apple devices. Techniques for decrypting encrypted iOS data involve leveraging various cryptographic methods and tools to access and recover protected information stored on Apple devices. Understanding these techniques is essential for forensic analysts, security researchers, and developers involved in data recovery and digital investigations. One of the primary approaches to decrypting iOS data is through the use of **Keychain Services**, which manages cryptographic keys and sensitive information securely on iOS devices. Developers and forensic experts can utilize Keychain Services APIs to access stored passwords, encryption keys, and certificates programmatically, enabling decryption of encrypted data protected by iOS's data protection mechanisms.

In forensic investigations, **Physical Acquisition** is a technique used to extract encrypted data directly from iOS devices' NAND flash memory. Tools like **Cellebrite UFED** and **GrayKey** facilitate physical acquisition by bypassing iOS's security measures and extracting a complete image of the device's storage, including encrypted data. This method enables forensic analysts to access encrypted app data, messages, and other sensitive information stored on the device, providing insights into user activities and communications.

Another approach involves **File System Extraction**, where forensic tools such as **XRY** and **Oxygen Forensic Detective** are employed to acquire a logical or file system-level image of the iOS device. By analyzing file system structures and metadata, forensic analysts can identify encrypted files and employ decryption techniques to recover their contents. Tools may integrate decryption capabilities for common file encryption formats used by iOS applications, enabling extraction of plaintext data from encrypted files recovered during forensic examinations.

For recovering encrypted iCloud backups, forensic investigators utilize **Elcomsoft Phone Breaker** and **Celebrite Physical Analyzer**, which can extract encrypted backup files from iCloud and attempt to decrypt them using acquired credentials or recovery keys. These tools employ brute-force attacks or exploit vulnerabilities in iOS backup encryption to retrieve plaintext data from iCloud backups, providing access to messages, photos, and app data stored in iCloud accounts associated with the iOS device.

In scenarios where developers need to decrypt app-specific data protected by iOS's encryption mechanisms, understanding **App Sandbox** and **Data Protection** policies is crucial. iOS applications can utilize **NSFileProtection** APIs to enforce data encryption for files stored in their sandboxes, ensuring confidentiality and integrity. Developers can specify data protection classes for files based on their sensitivity and operational requirements, using attributes like `NSFileProtectionComplete` or `NSFileProtectionNone` to control encryption behaviors and access restrictions.

Moreover, developers may implement **Custom Encryption Algorithms** within iOS applications to encrypt sensitive data using proprietary or industry-standard encryption schemes. By integrating encryption libraries like **CryptoSwift** or **CryptoKit**, developers can implement AES, RSA, or other encryption algorithms to protect user data stored locally or transmitted over networks. Custom encryption implementations should adhere to iOS security guidelines and best practices to ensure data confidentiality and prevent unauthorized access or tampering.

In the context of enterprise deployments, organizations utilize **Mobile Device Management (MDM)** solutions and **Enterprise Mobile Management (EMM)** platforms to manage encryption policies and securely deploy iOS devices within corporate environments. MDM solutions enable administrators to enforce encryption settings, configure secure communication channels using **VPN** and **Wi-Fi Security** configurations, and remotely wipe devices to protect sensitive data in case of loss or theft.

Furthermore, for developers and researchers focusing on iOS security assessments and vulnerability research, **Jailbreaking** is a technique that bypasses iOS's security restrictions to gain elevated privileges and access encrypted data. Tools like **checkra1n** and **unc0ver** exploit vulnerabilities in iOS to install custom firmware that circumvents Apple's security mechanisms, allowing researchers to analyze and decrypt protected data for security testing purposes.

In addition to software-based decryption techniques, hardware-based attacks such as **Fault Injection** and **Side-Channel Attacks** target iOS devices' hardware components to bypass encryption and access sensitive data. These advanced techniques require specialized equipment and expertise to manipulate device operation or exploit cryptographic implementation flaws, potentially compromising data protection mechanisms designed by Apple.

In summary, mastering techniques for decrypting encrypted iOS data requires a comprehensive understanding of iOS's cryptographic protocols, forensic methodologies, and security vulnerabilities. By leveraging tools and methods such as Keychain Services, physical acquisition, file system extraction, iCloud backup decryption, app sandbox analysis, custom encryption implementations, MDM solutions, jailbreaking, and advanced hardware attacks, analysts, developers, and researchers can effectively decrypt encrypted iOS data for forensic investigations, security assessments, and application development purposes, ensuring data security, privacy, and compliance with regulatory requirements in the evolving landscape of mobile device security.

# Chapter 4: Reverse Engineering iOS Applications

An overview of iOS application structure provides insight into the fundamental components and organization of applications developed for Apple's mobile operating system. iOS applications are packaged as bundles with a defined structure that includes executable code, resources, metadata, and configuration files. The core of an iOS app resides in its **.app** bundle, which is structured hierarchically to include the executable binary, compiled resources such as images, storyboards, and localization files, as well as metadata files like **Info.plist** that specify app configuration settings and permissions.

At the root level of an iOS application bundle, the **Info.plist** file serves as the main configuration file, containing essential metadata such as the app's bundle identifier, version number, supported device orientations, required capabilities, and permissions requested from the user. Developers configure these settings using Xcode's graphical interface or by directly editing the **Info.plist** file using a text editor or terminal commands like `plutil` to validate or convert property list files.

The **Executable** file within the .app bundle contains compiled machine code for the application's main executable binary, typically written in Objective-C or Swift. Developers compile and link their source code using Xcode's build system, generating an executable file that is bundled with the application and executed on iOS devices or simulators. Deployment commands like `xcodebuild` or `xcrun` manage the build process, compiling source code, linking libraries, and generating the executable binary for distribution or testing.

iOS applications utilize **Frameworks and Libraries** to modularize functionality and integrate pre-built components for features such as user interface elements, networking capabilities, and data storage. Frameworks like UIKit, Foundation, Core Data, and others provide APIs and classes for common tasks, enabling developers to build responsive, feature-rich applications efficiently. Xcode integrates frameworks using build phases and linking commands, ensuring dependencies are resolved and bundled within the .app package during the build process.

**Resources** in an iOS application include files such as images, icons, audio/video assets, localized strings, and Interface Builder (IB) files used to design user interfaces visually. These resources are stored within designated directories like **Assets.xcassets** for images and icons, **Base.lproj** for localization resources, and **Main.storyboard** or **.xib** files for defining app interfaces. Xcode manages these resources through project folders and asset catalogs, allowing developers to preview, organize, and reference resources programmatically or within Interface Builder.

The **Documents Directory** within an iOS application's sandboxed file system is where the app stores user-generated content, configuration files, and data files that need to persist between application sessions. Developers access the Documents directory programmatically using APIs like `FileManager.default.urls(for: .documentDirectory, in: .userDomainMask)` in Swift or `NSSearchPathForDirectoriesInDomains(NSDocumentDirectory, NSUserDomainMask, YES)` in Objective-C to retrieve the URL path for storing and retrieving application-specific files.

iOS applications are structured around the **App Sandbox**, a security mechanism that restricts each app's access to its own data and resources, ensuring user privacy and system integrity. The App Sandbox enforces file system isolation, network access controls, and inter-process communication restrictions, preventing unauthorized access to sensitive data and mitigating risks associated with malicious software or compromised applications. Developers configure App Sandbox entitlements using Xcode's capabilities editor or by editing the **Entitlements.plist** file to specify app permissions and access levels required for specific operations.

**Code Signing** is integral to iOS application structure and security, ensuring that apps distributed through the App Store or enterprise channels are verified and trusted by iOS devices. Developers sign their apps using

Xcode's **Signing & Capabilities** settings, which generate and manage cryptographic certificates and provisioning profiles issued by Apple's Developer Program. Code signing commands like `codesign` and `security` in the terminal validate app integrity, authenticate developer identities, and enable secure installation on iOS devices during deployment.

During **Deployment**, iOS applications undergo various stages, including development, testing on simulators or physical devices, and distribution through the App Store, TestFlight, or enterprise distribution channels. Xcode facilitates deployment workflows using provisioning profiles, App IDs, and developer certificates configured in the developer portal. Developers use Xcode's Archive feature or terminal commands like `xcodebuild` to build, archive, and export .ipa files for distribution, ensuring apps meet Apple's guidelines and undergo App Store review processes successfully.

**Version Control** and **Collaborative Development** are essential aspects of managing iOS application structure and codebase evolution. Developers use version control systems such as Git or SVN to track changes, collaborate with team members, and manage code branches effectively. Xcode integrates with Git repositories for source code management, enabling developers to commit, branch, merge changes, and resolve conflicts directly within the IDE, ensuring codebase consistency and version history tracking across development cycles.

iOS applications adhere to **Human Interface Guidelines** (HIG) to ensure consistent user experiences and design principles across Apple's ecosystem. Developers design app interfaces using Interface Builder or SwiftUI, following HIG recommendations for layout, typography, navigation, and interaction patterns. Xcode provides design tools, asset libraries, and preview features to visualize app interfaces and simulate user interactions, enabling developers to create intuitive, accessible, and visually appealing experiences for iOS users.

In summary, understanding the structured components and development practices of iOS applications is essential for developers aiming to build robust, secure, and user-friendly apps for Apple's mobile platform. By mastering tools, techniques, and best practices related to app bundling, resource management, file system access, security measures like App Sandbox and code signing, deployment workflows, version control, and adherence to Human Interface Guidelines, developers can create high-quality iOS applications that meet user expectations, comply with Apple's standards, and deliver seamless experiences on iOS devices. Methods for static and dynamic analysis are essential techniques employed in software development, cybersecurity, and quality assurance to evaluate the behavior, performance, and security of applications. **Static analysis** involves examining source code, binaries, or bytecode without executing the program, aiming to identify potential vulnerabilities, code quality issues, or compliance violations. Tools like **CodeQL** and **SonarQube** perform static analysis by parsing source code files, analyzing control flow, data flow, and variable usage to detect coding errors, security flaws, and adherence to coding standards. Developers integrate static analysis tools into CI/CD pipelines using commands like `codeql analyze` or `sonar-scanner` to automate code reviews and enforce coding best practices throughout the development lifecycle.

**Dynamic analysis**, on the other hand, evaluates application behavior during runtime by executing the software and monitoring its interactions with system resources, network communications, and user inputs. Tools such as **Burp Suite**, **Wireshark**, and **Fiddler** conduct dynamic analysis by capturing and analyzing network traffic, identifying security vulnerabilities like SQL injection or cross-site scripting (XSS) attacks. Security analysts deploy dynamic analysis tools by configuring proxies or intercepting traffic using commands like `burpsuite` or `wireshark` to inspect HTTP requests and responses, pinpointing potential vulnerabilities for remediation.

**Penetration testing** combines both static and dynamic analysis techniques to assess an application's security posture comprehensively. Penetration testers utilize tools like **Metasploit** or **Nmap** to conduct vulnerability assessments, exploit security weaknesses, and simulate cyberattacks to evaluate an application's resilience against real-world threats. Command-line interfaces (`msfconsole` for Metasploit, `nmap` for Nmap) enable penetration testers to execute scans, exploit vulnerabilities, and generate detailed reports on identified security issues, assisting organizations in prioritizing remediation efforts and strengthening their defenses.

In software development, **linting** tools like **ESLint** for JavaScript or **Pylint** for Python perform static analysis to enforce coding style guidelines, detect syntax errors, and optimize code readability. Developers integrate linters into their IDEs or CI/CD pipelines using commands such as `eslint` or `pylint` to automate code formatting checks and maintain code consistency across projects, improving code quality and reducing maintenance overhead.

For **mobile application security**, **Mobile Device Management (MDM)** solutions and **Mobile Application Management (MAM)** platforms employ static and dynamic analysis techniques to assess app security, monitor device compliance, and enforce security policies. MDM/MAM administrators deploy mobile security solutions like **Microsoft Intune** or **VMware Workspace ONE** to perform static app scans (`Intune app protection policies`) and dynamic app behavior analysis (`Workspace ONE UEM Tunnel`) to protect corporate data and mitigate risks associated with mobile device usage in enterprise environments.

In **malware analysis** and **reverse engineering**, analysts use static and dynamic analysis techniques to analyze suspicious files, identify malicious behaviors, and develop countermeasures to mitigate cyber threats. Tools like **IDA Pro** and **Ghidra** assist analysts in dissecting binaries (`ida64` or `ghidraRun`) to understand code execution flow, identify encryption algorithms (`CryptDecrypt`), and uncover hidden functionalities (`Ghidra Decompiler`), facilitating the detection and containment of malware infections.

**Web application security testing** relies on static and dynamic analysis methodologies to assess vulnerabilities (`OWASP ZAP` or `Arachni`), identify injection flaws (`ZAP CLI`), and validate input sanitization (`Arachni --checks=xss,sql_injection`), ensuring robust protection against web-based attacks. Security testers automate web security scans using CLI tools (`zap-cli` or `arachni_scan`) to discover vulnerabilities (`OWASP Top 10`) and remediate security weaknesses (`Arachni --report=json`), enhancing the resilience of web applications against cyber threats.

**Behavioral analysis** techniques like **sandboxing** and **emulation** simulate application environments (`Cuckoo Sandbox` or `QEMU`) to observe program behavior (`cuckoo` or `qemu`) and detect malicious activities (`API hooking`, `file system changes`), enabling analysts to analyze malware (`cuckoo submit sample.exe`) and assess potential risks (`qemu -hda disk.img`), enhancing threat intelligence (`malware analysis reports`) and incident response (`sandbox analysis`).

**Performance profiling** tools (`Xcode Instruments` or `VisualVM`) conduct dynamic analysis (`instruments`) of application performance metrics (`heap memory`, `CPU usage`), identifying bottlenecks (`time profiling`) and optimizing resource utilization (`heap allocation`), ensuring optimal app performance (`thread analysis`) and responsiveness (`visualvm`).

**Machine learning** (`TensorFlow` or `PyTorch`) leverages static and dynamic analysis techniques (`tf.data.Dataset` or `torch.nn.Module`) to train (`model.fit`) and deploy (`torchscript`) AI models (`tf.keras`) for predictive analytics (`tf.data`) and anomaly detection (`torch.autograd`), enhancing decision-making (`machine learning models`) and automation (`model deployment`).

In **cloud computing**, `AWS CloudTrail` and `Azure Monitor` perform static and dynamic analysis (`cloudtrail` or `az monitor`) to monitor (`cloudwatch`) and analyze (`log analytics`) cloud infrastructure (`vpc flow logs`) and services (`application insights`), ensuring compliance (`audit logs`) and security (`threat detection`).

**Chapter 5: Analyzing Malware and Suspicious Activities**

Detecting and analyzing iOS malware requires a comprehensive approach that integrates both technical expertise and sophisticated tools. iOS, known for its stringent security measures, faces evolving threats that necessitate proactive detection strategies. One effective method involves leveraging static analysis techniques on suspicious applications. By examining the binary code using tools like `class-dump` or `Hopper Disassembler`, analysts can uncover potential malicious behaviors embedded within the app's structure. Additionally, dynamic analysis plays a crucial role in understanding malware's runtime behavior. Tools such as `Cycript` enable researchers to interact with an app while it runs, revealing hidden functionalities or unauthorized data access. Moreover, network traffic analysis using tools like `Wireshark` or `tcpdump` provides insights into suspicious data transmissions initiated by malicious apps. This method helps identify communication channels used by malware to exfiltrate sensitive information or receive commands from remote servers. Furthermore, sandboxing techniques simulate the iOS environment to observe malware behavior in a controlled setting. Tools like `Apple's Xcode Instruments` facilitate detailed performance monitoring and behavior analysis, aiding in the identification of anomalous activities indicative of malware presence. Moreover, behavioral analysis techniques focus on app actions post-installation, monitoring for unusual activities such as unauthorized access to contacts or device resources. By scrutinizing system logs (`syslog`) and application logs (`asl`), analysts can trace malicious activities and establish a timeline of events for forensic investigation. Additionally, memory forensics using tools like `iLEAPP` or `Mobius Forensic Toolkit` allows extraction and analysis of volatile data from iOS devices, uncovering artifacts left behind by malware during runtime. Moreover, establishing a robust threat intelligence framework facilitates early detection of emerging iOS malware strains. Continuous monitoring of reputable sources such as CVE databases and security forums provides timely updates on known vulnerabilities and threat indicators relevant to iOS. Additionally, collaborating with industry peers and participating in information-sharing communities enhances situational awareness and accelerates mitigation efforts against evolving threats. Moreover, leveraging machine learning algorithms for anomaly detection enhances the capability to identify new and previously unknown iOS malware variants. By training models on large datasets of benign and malicious app behaviors, organizations can automate the detection process and prioritize responses to potential threats effectively. Furthermore, understanding the attack vectors commonly exploited by iOS malware enhances defensive strategies. Techniques such as phishing via malicious links or social engineering tactics exploit user trust to trick them into installing compromised apps. Educating users about safe app installation practices and encouraging them to verify app permissions mitigates the risk of inadvertently downloading malicious software. Additionally, app vetting procedures and code reviews during the development phase ensure adherence to secure coding practices and minimize the introduction of vulnerabilities into iOS applications. Moreover, maintaining a secure app ecosystem through timely patching and updates mitigates known vulnerabilities exploited by iOS malware. Regularly applying iOS security patches released by Apple and enforcing strict app review guidelines for the App Store ecosystem mitigate the risk of widespread malware infections. Furthermore, incident response planning tailored to iOS malware incidents ensures swift containment and mitigation of potential damage. Establishing predefined procedures for isolating compromised devices, preserving forensic evidence, and restoring from secure backups minimizes disruption to operations and protects sensitive data. Additionally, conducting post-incident reviews and implementing lessons learned enhances future incident response capabilities against evolving iOS malware threats. Ultimately, combating iOS malware requires a proactive and multifaceted approach that integrates advanced detection techniques, continuous monitoring, user education, and collaborative threat intelligence. By staying vigilant and leveraging specialized tools and expertise, organizations can effectively defend against the growing sophistication of iOS malware and safeguard sensitive information on Apple devices. Investigating suspicious app behavior is a critical aspect of cybersecurity, particularly in identifying potential threats and safeguarding systems from malicious activities. When faced with an app exhibiting unusual or unauthorized actions on a device, analysts employ various techniques to conduct a thorough investigation. One fundamental approach involves conducting static analysis of the app's binary code using tools such as `class-dump` or `Hopper Disassembler`. These tools enable analysts to inspect the app's structure and identify any hidden functionalities or suspicious code segments that could indicate malicious intent. Moreover, dynamic analysis plays a pivotal role in understanding the app's behavior in real-time. Tools like `Cycript` allow analysts to interact with the app during runtime, enabling them to uncover runtime behaviors, monitor API calls, and detect any anomalous activities that might suggest malicious behavior. Additionally, network traffic analysis using tools such as `Wireshark` or `tcpdump` helps in examining the app's communication patterns. By capturing and analyzing network traffic generated by the app, analysts can detect unauthorized data transmissions, identify command-and-control servers, and understand the scope of potential data exfiltration. Furthermore, sandboxing techniques are employed to isolate and observe the app's behavior in a controlled environment. This method involves executing the app within a virtualized sandbox to monitor its interactions with the operating system and other apps, thereby detecting any attempts to access sensitive data or exploit system vulnerabilities. Additionally, behavioral analysis techniques focus on monitoring the app's actions post-installation. By reviewing system logs (`syslog`) and application logs (`asl`), analysts can trace the app's activities, identify any suspicious processes or file modifications, and establish a timeline of events to reconstruct the sequence of actions taken by the app. Moreover, memory forensics tools such as `iLEAPP` or `Mobius Forensic Toolkit` are utilized to extract and analyze volatile data from the device's memory. This enables analysts to uncover artifacts left behind by the app during runtime, including cached data, temporary files, and remnants of executed processes, providing valuable insights into the app's behavior and potential security implications. Additionally, leveraging machine learning algorithms for anomaly detection enhances the capability to identify deviations from normal app behavior. By training models on historical data of benign and malicious app behaviors, organizations can automate the detection process and promptly flag suspicious activities for further investigation. Furthermore, understanding the attack vectors commonly exploited by malicious apps enhances defensive strategies. Techniques such as privilege escalation, data exfiltration, or unauthorized access to device resources are often indicative of malicious intent. Educating users about safe app installation practices, such as downloading from trusted sources and verifying app permissions, helps mitigate the risk of inadvertently installing malicious apps. Moreover, conducting thorough app vetting procedures and code reviews during the development phase ensures adherence to secure coding practices and reduces the likelihood of introducing vulnerabilities into apps. Regularly applying security patches and updates released by app developers or platform providers mitigates known vulnerabilities exploited by malicious apps. Additionally, incident response planning tailored to app behavior anomalies ensures swift containment and mitigation of potential damage. Establishing predefined procedures for isolating compromised devices, preserving forensic evidence, and restoring from secure backups minimizes disruption to operations and safeguards sensitive data. Moreover, conducting post-incident reviews and implementing lessons learned enhances future incident response capabilities against emerging threats. Ultimately, investigating suspicious app behavior demands a proactive approach that integrates advanced analysis techniques, continuous monitoring, user education, and collaborative threat intelligence. By staying vigilant and leveraging specialized tools and expertise, organizations can effectively detect and mitigate the risks posed by malicious apps, thereby protecting sensitive information and ensuring the integrity of their systems.

## Chapter 6: Incident Response in iOS Forensics

Steps and procedures for iOS incident response are crucial for promptly identifying, containing, and mitigating security breaches on Apple devices. When an incident occurs, the initial step involves establishing incident response readiness by having a documented plan that outlines roles, responsibilities, and communication protocols among incident response team members. This plan should include procedures for identifying and categorizing incidents based on severity and impact, enabling swift prioritization of response efforts. Utilizing Apple's Device Enrollment Program (DEP) or Apple Configurator facilitates the deployment of consistent device configurations and security policies across the organization, ensuring all devices adhere to baseline security standards. Furthermore, upon detecting a potential security breach, the first action is to isolate the affected iOS device from the network to prevent further compromise and preserve volatile data for forensic analysis using techniques such as `iLEAPP` or `Mobius Forensic Toolkit` to extract and analyze artifacts from the device's memory. Additionally, capturing system logs (`syslog`) and application logs (`asl`) helps establish a timeline of events leading up to and following the incident, aiding in the reconstruction of the attack chain and identification of unauthorized activities.

In cases where malicious apps or unauthorized software are suspected, performing static analysis using tools like `class-dump` or `Hopper Disassembler` allows for a detailed examination of the app's binary code to uncover hidden functionalities or suspicious code segments indicative of malicious intent. Moreover, conducting dynamic analysis with tools such as `Cycript` enables real-time interaction with the app to monitor runtime behaviors, API calls, and potential exploitation attempts. Network traffic analysis using `Wireshark` or `tcpdump` assists in identifying communication channels utilized by malicious apps to exfiltrate data or communicate with remote command-and-control servers, providing insights into the scope and impact of the incident.

Implementing sandboxing techniques to simulate the iOS environment aids in observing the behavior of suspicious apps in a controlled setting, allowing for the identification of unauthorized data access or system exploitation attempts. Furthermore, leveraging machine learning algorithms for anomaly detection enhances the capability to detect and respond to unusual activities or deviations from normal device behavior, automating the identification of potential threats. Educating users about safe app installation practices, such as downloading from trusted sources and verifying app permissions, reduces the risk of inadvertently installing malicious apps and strengthens overall security posture.

Regularly updating iOS devices with security patches and updates released by Apple mitigates known vulnerabilities exploited by malicious actors, reducing the attack surface and enhancing device resilience. Additionally, conducting thorough app vetting procedures and code reviews during the development phase ensures adherence to secure coding practices, minimizing the introduction of vulnerabilities into iOS applications. Implementing incident response playbooks tailored to iOS security incidents ensures consistent and effective response efforts, enabling rapid containment and mitigation of security breaches.

Establishing a secure backup strategy for iOS devices facilitates data recovery and restoration in the event of a security incident, minimizing disruption to operations and preserving critical information. Moreover, establishing a secure backup strategy for iOS devices facilitates data recovery and restoration in the event of a security incident, minimizing disruption to operations and preserving critical information. Case management in iOS forensic incidents is a structured process that encompasses several key phases, each essential for effectively investigating and resolving security breaches on Apple devices. The initial step involves incident identification, where organizations deploy monitoring tools and security controls such as Mobile Device Management (MDM) solutions or Endpoint Detection and Response (EDR) systems to detect anomalous activities or unauthorized access attempts. Upon detecting a potential incident, the immediate action is to isolate the affected iOS device from the network using commands like disabling Wi-Fi (`settings set wifiautojoin 0`) or turning off cellular data (`settings set mobiledata 0`), preventing further compromise and preserving volatile data crucial for forensic analysis.

Capturing volatile data using tools like `iLEAPP` or `Mobius Forensic Toolkit` enables forensic investigators to extract artifacts from the device's memory, including active processes, network connections, and cached information, providing insights into the state of the device at the time of the incident. Concurrently, capturing system logs (`syslog`) and application logs (`asl`) aids in establishing a timeline of events leading up to and following the incident, essential for reconstructing the attack chain and understanding the impact on device integrity and data confidentiality. Analyzing these logs using commands like `log show --predicate 'subsystem == "com.apple.Security"' --info` filters for security-related entries, revealing potential indicators of compromise (IOCs) or suspicious activities.

In cases involving suspected malicious apps or unauthorized software, conducting static analysis with tools like `class-dump` or `Hopper Disassembler` allows forensic analysts to examine the app's binary code, identifying hidden functionalities or malicious code segments indicative of security threats. Dynamic analysis techniques using `Cycript` facilitate real-time interaction with the app during runtime, monitoring API calls, data storage, and behavior patterns that may reveal malicious intent or unauthorized actions. Network traffic analysis using tools such as `Wireshark` or `tcpdump` captures and inspects network communications originating from the device, identifying communication channels used by malicious apps for data exfiltration or command-and-control activities, crucial for understanding the scope and impact of the incident.

Implementing sandboxing techniques to simulate the iOS environment isolates suspicious apps, allowing forensic investigators to observe their behavior in a controlled setting without compromising the integrity of other apps or system resources. This method helps identify unauthorized data access, system exploitation attempts, or interactions with sensitive device functionalities. Leveraging machine learning algorithms for anomaly detection enhances the capability to detect deviations from normal device behavior, automating the identification of potential threats and expediting response efforts.

Educating users on secure app installation practices, such as downloading from trusted sources and scrutinizing app permissions, mitigates the risk of inadvertently installing malicious apps and strengthens overall device security. Regularly updating iOS devices with security patches and updates released by Apple mitigates known vulnerabilities exploited by malicious actors, reducing the attack surface and enhancing device resilience against emerging threats. Conducting thorough app vetting procedures and code reviews during the development phase ensures adherence to secure coding practices, minimizing the introduction of vulnerabilities into iOS applications.

Establishing incident response playbooks tailored to iOS forensic incidents streamlines response efforts, ensuring consistent and effective handling of security breaches. These playbooks outline predefined procedures for incident detection, containment, eradication, and recovery, facilitating swift and coordinated action to minimize disruption to operations and mitigate potential damage. Maintaining secure backups of iOS devices and critical data facilitates rapid restoration in the event of data loss or device compromise, preserving business continuity and minimizing financial and reputational risks.

Moreover, documenting all phases of the forensic investigation and incident response process is essential for legal and regulatory compliance, ensuring transparency and accountability in handling sensitive information and security breaches. Collaborating with legal counsel and law enforcement, when necessary, ensures adherence to legal requirements and facilitates the preservation of evidence for potential criminal or civil proceedings. Conducting post-incident reviews and lessons learned sessions enhances organizational resilience and improves incident response capabilities against evolving iOS security threats.

Ultimately, effective case management in iOS forensic incidents demands a proactive and multidisciplinary approach that integrates advanced forensic techniques, continuous monitoring, user education, and collaborative partnerships with internal stakeholders and external experts. By adopting a structured and systematic approach to incident response, organizations can effectively safeguard Apple devices, protect sensitive information, and mitigate the impact of security breaches on their operations and reputation.

# Chapter 7: Advanced Network Forensics on iOS Devices

Techniques for capturing and analyzing iOS network traffic are essential for understanding app behaviors, detecting potential security threats, and ensuring data privacy on Apple devices. One effective method involves using tools like `Wireshark` or `tcpdump` to intercept and capture network packets transmitted to and from an iOS device. Deploying `tcpdump` with specific filters, such as `tcpdump -i en0 -s 0 -w capture.pcap`, captures all packets on interface `en0` without truncation, providing a comprehensive view of network communications. This approach enables forensic analysts to inspect packet headers and payloads, identifying communication protocols, destinations, and potential anomalies indicative of malicious activities.

Furthermore, conducting packet analysis with `Wireshark` allows for in-depth inspection of captured packets, facilitating the identification of HTTP requests, API calls, and encrypted traffic exchanged between iOS apps and remote servers. Using `Wireshark`'s built-in filters, such as `http.request.method == "POST"`, analysts can isolate specific types of network activities, uncovering unauthorized data transmissions or suspicious command-and-control communications. Moreover, decrypting SSL/TLS traffic using `Wireshark`'s decryption feature or `SSLKEYLOGFILE` environment variable enables visibility into encrypted communications, essential for detecting malware that attempts to conceal its activities through encryption.

Another technique involves utilizing `mitmproxy` to intercept and analyze HTTPS traffic originating from iOS apps. By configuring iOS devices to trust the `mitmproxy` certificate authority (CA) and redirecting traffic through a proxy server, analysts can capture and inspect decrypted HTTP/HTTPS requests and responses in real-time. This method provides insights into app behaviors, API interactions, and data exchanges that may indicate security vulnerabilities or compliance violations. Additionally, `mitmproxy`'s scripting capabilities allow for custom analysis and manipulation of intercepted traffic, enhancing forensic investigations by extracting relevant metadata or identifying patterns of suspicious behavior.

Implementing network traffic analysis within a controlled environment, such as a virtualized sandbox or network emulator, facilitates the observation of iOS app behaviors under simulated conditions. Tools like `Charles Proxy` or `Burp Suite` intercept and analyze HTTP/HTTPS traffic, allowing analysts to monitor app interactions with external servers, capture session cookies, and identify potential data leakage or unauthorized access attempts. Configuring iOS devices to route traffic through a proxy server controlled by `Charles Proxy` or `Burp Suite` enables real-time inspection of app communications, aiding in the detection of vulnerabilities or compliance violations.

Moreover, integrating network traffic analysis into incident response procedures enhances the capability to detect and respond to security incidents involving iOS devices. Capturing and analyzing network logs (`pcap`) and session data (`har`) using tools like `tshark` or `Fiddler` provides a detailed audit trail of network activities, facilitating forensic investigations and compliance audits. Analyzing DNS query logs with `tshark -i eth0 -nn -l -f 'port 53' -T fields -e dns.qry.name` helps identify suspicious domain name resolutions indicative of malware command-and-control communications or phishing attacks targeting iOS users.

Furthermore, leveraging machine learning algorithms for anomaly detection enhances the capability to identify deviations from normal network traffic patterns on iOS devices. By training models on historical data of benign and malicious network behaviors, organizations can automate the detection of anomalous activities, such as unusual spikes in data transfers or unauthorized access attempts, prompting timely investigation and response. Educating users about safe browsing habits and the risks associated with unsecured Wi-Fi networks reduces the likelihood of exposing iOS devices to malicious network threats, reinforcing overall security posture.

Regularly updating iOS devices with the latest security patches and firmware releases issued by Apple mitigates known vulnerabilities exploited by malicious actors, reducing the attack surface and enhancing device resilience against emerging threats. Additionally, conducting vulnerability assessments and penetration testing of iOS apps and network infrastructure identifies potential security weaknesses, enabling proactive remediation and risk mitigation strategies. Collaborating with cybersecurity experts and sharing threat intelligence within the industry enhances situational awareness and improves defense capabilities against evolving network-based threats targeting iOS platforms.

Ultimately, mastering techniques for capturing and analyzing iOS network traffic requires a combination of technical expertise, specialized tools, and proactive security measures. By implementing robust network traffic analysis practices and integrating them into comprehensive cybersecurity frameworks, organizations can effectively safeguard data privacy, detect security breaches, and maintain the integrity of iOS devices in an increasingly interconnected digital landscape. Investigating network-based attacks on iOS devices requires a systematic approach that integrates advanced forensic techniques, specialized tools, and comprehensive knowledge of iOS security vulnerabilities. When confronted with suspected network-based attacks targeting iOS devices, the initial step is to isolate the affected device from the network using commands such as disabling Wi-Fi (`settings set wifiautojoin 0`) or turning off cellular data (`settings set mobiledata 0`), preventing further communication with malicious servers or compromised networks and preserving volatile data crucial for forensic analysis. Capturing network traffic using tools like `tcpdump` facilitates the collection of packet captures (`pcap`) on iOS devices, allowing forensic analysts to examine communication protocols, data exchanges, and potential indicators of compromise (IOCs) through commands like `tcpdump -i en0 -s 0 -w capture.pcap`.

Moreover, analyzing captured network packets with `Wireshark` enables detailed inspection of HTTP/HTTPS requests, DNS queries, and encrypted traffic, using filters like `http.request.method == "POST"` to isolate suspicious activities indicative of data exfiltration or command-and-control communications. Decrypting SSL/TLS traffic within `Wireshark` using the `SSLKEYLOGFILE` environment variable or `Wireshark`'s built-in decryption feature provides visibility into encrypted communications, essential for identifying malware that attempts to conceal its actions through encryption.

Employing `mitmproxy` for HTTPS interception and analysis allows forensic investigators to capture decrypted traffic originating from iOS apps by configuring the iOS device to trust the `mitmproxy` certificate authority (CA) and redirecting traffic through a proxy server. This technique facilitates real-time monitoring and inspection of app behaviors, API interactions, and data exchanges, enabling the detection of security vulnerabilities or compliance violations. Leveraging `mitmproxy`'s scripting capabilities enhances forensic investigations by extracting metadata, identifying patterns of suspicious behavior, and manipulating intercepted traffic for detailed analysis.

Furthermore, conducting DNS query analysis with tools like `tshark` (`tshark -i eth0 -nn -l -f 'port 53' -T fields -e dns.qry.name`) aids in identifying domain name resolutions associated with malicious activities, such as phishing campaigns or malware command-and-control communications targeting iOS devices. Analyzing DNS logs helps forensic analysts trace the origins of network-based attacks, understand the scope of the compromise, and prioritize response efforts accordingly.

Integrating network traffic analysis into incident response procedures strengthens the capability to detect and mitigate network-based attacks on iOS devices. Analyzing network logs (`pcap`) and session data (`har`) with tools like `tshark` or `Fiddler` provides a comprehensive audit trail of network activities, facilitating forensic investigations, compliance audits, and legal proceedings by command `fiddler` for better analysis. Employing machine learning algorithms for anomaly detection enhances the ability to identify abnormal network traffic patterns on iOS devices, automating the detection of suspicious activities such as unauthorized data transfers or unusual network behaviors. By training machine learning models on historical data of benign and malicious network behaviors, organizations can proactively detect and respond to network-based attacks targeting iOS platforms.

Educating iOS users about safe browsing habits and the risks associated with unsecured Wi-Fi networks reduces the likelihood of falling victim to network-based attacks. Regularly updating iOS devices with the latest security patches and firmware releases issued by Apple mitigates known vulnerabilities exploited by malicious actors, enhancing device resilience against emerging threats. Conducting vulnerability assessments and penetration testing of iOS apps and network infrastructure identifies potential security weaknesses, enabling organizations to implement proactive remediation and risk mitigation strategies. Collaborating with cybersecurity experts and sharing threat intelligence within the industry enhances situational awareness and improves defense capabilities against evolving network-based threats targeting iOS platforms.

Ultimately, investigating network-based attacks on iOS devices demands a multidisciplinary approach that combines technical expertise, specialized tools, proactive security measures, and continuous vigilance. By mastering advanced forensic techniques for capturing and analyzing network traffic, organizations can effectively safeguard data privacy, detect security breaches, and maintain the integrity of iOS devices in an increasingly interconnected digital landscape

## Chapter 8: Case Study: Corporate Espionage Investigation

In the realm of corporate espionage, a case unfolds as a complex web of clandestine operations, strategic maneuvers, and high-stakes intelligence gathering aimed at gaining competitive advantage through illicit means. Such cases often begin with subtle indicators and suspicions rather than overt actions, prompting organizations to deploy sophisticated monitoring tools and surveillance techniques to detect anomalies in their network traffic or employee behavior. Employing tools like `tcpdump` to capture network packets and `Wireshark` for detailed packet analysis, investigators meticulously trace the origins of suspicious activities, examining communication patterns and identifying unauthorized access attempts or data exfiltration efforts. These tools provide a crucial digital footprint that forms the foundation of the investigative process, enabling forensic experts to reconstruct timelines, identify potential perpetrators, and understand the methods employed to breach corporate defenses.

Moreover, in cases where intellectual property theft is suspected, forensic analysts employ specialized techniques such as memory forensics using `Volatility Framework` or `iLEAPP` to extract volatile data from compromised devices, uncovering artifacts that reveal unauthorized access to proprietary information or trade secrets. These artifacts serve as key pieces of evidence in legal proceedings and assist in establishing the extent of data compromise and the financial impact on the affected organization. Furthermore, leveraging `mitmproxy` for HTTPS interception and analysis helps investigators capture decrypted traffic originating from suspicious applications or devices, providing insights into communication channels used for covert information exchange or unauthorized surveillance activities.

The investigative process often extends beyond technical analysis to include comprehensive digital forensic examinations of corporate devices and network infrastructure. Conducting thorough examinations with tools like `Autopsy` or `Encase` allows forensic experts to recover deleted files, analyze system logs, and trace user activities, uncovering hidden traces of espionage operations or insider threats. This meticulous approach is essential for piecing together the puzzle of corporate espionage, identifying the motives behind malicious actions, and determining whether they were driven by internal collaborators or external entities seeking to gain a competitive edge in the market.

Additionally, collaborating with law enforcement agencies and legal counsel becomes imperative in cases of corporate espionage, as it involves navigating complex legal landscapes and ensuring adherence to regulatory requirements. Providing law enforcement agencies with detailed forensic reports and evidence obtained through tools like `tshark` for network traffic analysis or `Fiddler` for HTTP/HTTPS interception strengthens the case against perpetrators and supports legal actions aimed at prosecuting those responsible for espionage activities. Moreover, engaging in threat intelligence sharing initiatives within industry forums or cybersecurity communities enhances organizational resilience against future espionage attempts, enabling proactive defense strategies and threat mitigation efforts.

Educating employees about corporate espionage risks and implementing robust security awareness programs helps mitigate insider threats and unauthorized information disclosure. By raising awareness about the importance of safeguarding sensitive information and recognizing suspicious activities, organizations can empower employees to become vigilant against social engineering tactics or unauthorized data access attempts orchestrated by malicious actors. Furthermore, implementing stringent access controls, encryption protocols, and multi-factor authentication mechanisms strengthens defenses against unauthorized data exfiltration and protects intellectual property from exploitation by adversaries seeking to undermine corporate competitiveness.

Forensic analysis and findings play a pivotal role in unraveling mysteries and solving complex cases across various domains, from criminal investigations to cybersecurity incidents and corporate disputes. In the realm of digital forensics, the process begins with the acquisition of evidence using tools such as `dd` or `FTK

Imager` to create forensic images of storage devices or digital media, ensuring the preservation of data integrity and chain of custody. Commands like `dd if=/dev/sda of=image.dd bs=1M` are employed to create a bit-by-bit copy (`image.dd`) of a source device (`/dev/sda`) with a specified block size (`bs=1M`), enabling forensic investigators to extract and analyze data without altering the original source.

Once the forensic image is obtained, analysts proceed with data extraction and examination using specialized tools like `Autopsy` or `Encase`, which facilitate file system analysis, keyword searches, and timeline reconstruction of digital artifacts. These tools enable investigators to uncover deleted files, browser history, chat logs, and other digital traces that provide insights into user activities and potential evidence of illicit behavior or criminal activity. Command-line utilities such as `grep` or `find` are utilized to search for specific keywords or patterns within forensic images, aiding in the identification of relevant information critical to the investigation.

Moreover, memory forensics techniques using tools like `Volatility Framework` enable analysts to capture and analyze volatile data from live systems or memory dumps (`memdump`), revealing running processes, open network connections, and artifacts indicative of malicious activities or intrusion attempts. Commands such as `volatility -f memdump.raw imageinfo` provide a comprehensive overview of the memory dump (`memdump.raw`), including the operating system version, memory profile, and potential volatility plugins for further analysis (`imageinfo`), aiding in the identification of memory artifacts relevant to the investigation.

In cases involving network breaches or cyberattacks, network forensics tools such as `tcpdump` or `Wireshark` are utilized to capture and analyze network traffic (`pcap` files), allowing investigators to reconstruct communication patterns, identify attack vectors, and pinpoint compromised systems or malicious actors. Commands like `tcpdump -i eth0 -w capture.pcap` capture network packets on interface `eth0` and write (`-w`) them to a file (`capture.pcap`), enabling detailed analysis of packet headers, payloads, and communication protocols used during the incident.

Additionally, email forensics tools like `MailXaminer` or `MailParser` assist in analyzing email headers, attachments, and metadata to trace the origins of phishing campaigns, identify spoofed email addresses, and establish communication links between perpetrators and victims. These tools extract email artifacts from forensic images or email archives, providing forensic examiners with valuable evidence of communication patterns, social engineering tactics, and malicious intent behind cyber incidents. Command-line utilities such as `exiftool` or `foremost` are employed to extract metadata or recover deleted files from email attachments, facilitating the reconstruction of email communications and identifying potential evidence relevant to the investigation.

Furthermore, mobile device forensics techniques involve extracting and analyzing data from smartphones or tablets using tools like `Cellebrite UFED` or `Oxygen Forensic Detective`, which support the acquisition of device backups (`iTunes` or `iCloud`), physical images (`.img` files), and logical extractions (`.tar` files). These tools enable investigators to recover call logs, text messages, GPS coordinates, and application data stored on mobile devices, providing insights into user activities, geographical movements, and communication networks relevant to criminal investigations or legal proceedings.

In corporate environments, forensic analysis plays a crucial role in investigating internal fraud, employee misconduct, or intellectual property theft. Utilizing digital forensic techniques, organizations can scrutinize employee workstations, email communications, and file servers to detect unauthorized access, data breaches, or insider threats. Command-line utilities such as `diff` or `md5sum` compare file hashes or directory structures between forensic images and live systems, verifying data integrity and identifying discrepancies that may indicate tampering or unauthorized modifications.

Moreover, forensic accounting techniques leverage digital evidence to trace financial transactions, analyze electronic payment records, and uncover discrepancies in financial statements. By examining digital artifacts such as spreadsheets, databases, and transaction logs, forensic accountants can identify patterns of fraudulent activity, embezzlement schemes, or money laundering operations within organizations. Command-line tools like `sqlite3` or `xlsx2csv` extract data from SQLite databases or Excel spreadsheets, enabling forensic accountants to analyze financial records, audit trails, and transaction histories relevant to financial investigations.

Ultimately, forensic analysis and findings provide critical insights into complex cases, guiding investigators, legal professionals, and organizations in making informed decisions based on digital evidence. By employing advanced forensic techniques, leveraging specialized tools, and adhering to rigorous investigative methodologies, forensic examiners can unravel the truth behind criminal activities, cybersecurity incidents, corporate disputes, and financial fraud schemes, ensuring justice, accountability, and safeguarding organizational integrity

## Chapter 9: Case Study: Digital Forensics in Law Enforcement

The role of digital forensics in law enforcement is pivotal in modern crime investigation, encompassing a range of techniques and technologies essential for gathering, analyzing, and presenting digital evidence in legal proceedings. At the forefront of digital forensic investigations, law enforcement agencies utilize tools such as `EnCase Forensic` or `AccessData FTK` to acquire forensic images (`.e01` or `.aff` files) of storage devices from crime scenes or suspects' premises, ensuring the preservation of data integrity and maintaining a documented chain of custody. Commands like `dc3dd` or `dd` are employed to create bit-for-bit copies (`dd if=/dev/sda of=image.dd bs=1M`) of hard drives (`/dev/sda`) with specified block sizes (`bs=1M`), facilitating forensic analysis without altering original data.

Upon acquiring forensic images, forensic examiners proceed with data extraction and analysis using tools like `Autopsy` or `X-Ways Forensics`, which facilitate file system analysis, keyword searches, and metadata examination to uncover digital evidence such as documents, photos, emails, and browser history. Command-line utilities such as `grep` or `find` are utilized to search for specific patterns (`grep -i "keyword" file.txt`) within forensic images or extracted data, aiding in the identification of relevant information crucial to the investigation.

Memory forensics techniques using tools like `Volatility Framework` enable investigators to analyze volatile data from live systems or memory dumps (`memdump`), revealing running processes, network connections, and artifacts indicative of malware infections or unauthorized access attempts. Commands like `volatility -f memdump.raw imageinfo` provide detailed information about memory dumps (`memdump.raw`), including the operating system version, memory profile, and potential volatility plugins (`imageinfo`), facilitating the identification of memory artifacts pertinent to the investigation.

In cases involving network-based crimes, network forensics tools such as `tcpdump` or `Wireshark` capture and analyze network traffic (`pcap` files), allowing investigators to reconstruct communication patterns, identify attack vectors, and trace digital footprints left by perpetrators. Commands like `tcpdump -i eth0 -w capture.pcap` capture network packets on interface `eth0` and write (`-w`) them to a file (`capture.pcap`), enabling detailed analysis of packet headers, payloads, and communication protocols used during the incident.

Email forensics tools like `MailXaminer` or `MailParser` assist in analyzing email headers, attachments, and metadata to trace the origins of phishing campaigns, identify spoofed email addresses, and establish communication links between suspects and accomplices. These tools extract email artifacts from forensic images or email archives, providing investigators with critical evidence of communication patterns, social engineering tactics, and criminal intent behind cyber incidents. Command-line utilities such as `exiftool` or `foremost` recover deleted files from email attachments or extract metadata, aiding in the reconstruction of email communications relevant to the investigation.

Mobile device forensics techniques involve extracting and analyzing data from smartphones or tablets using tools like `Cellebrite UFED` or `Oxygen Forensic Detective`, which support the acquisition of device backups (`iTunes` or `iCloud`), physical images (`.img` files), and logical extractions (`.tar` files). These tools enable investigators to recover call logs, text messages, GPS coordinates, and application data stored on mobile devices, providing insights into suspects' activities, geographical movements, and communication networks relevant to criminal investigations.

In addition to technical expertise and specialized tools, collaboration with legal professionals and adherence to strict procedural guidelines are essential in digital forensic investigations. Digital evidence obtained through forensic analysis must adhere to legal standards of admissibility, ensuring its relevance, authenticity, and integrity in court. Providing detailed forensic reports and expert testimony based on credible digital evidence strengthens the case against suspects and supports legal proceedings aimed at securing convictions or exonerations.

Moreover, digital forensics plays a crucial role in combating cybercrimes, fraud, child exploitation, and terrorism, providing law enforcement agencies with the necessary tools and capabilities to investigate, prosecute, and deter criminal activities in the digital age. By leveraging advanced forensic techniques, collaborating with international law enforcement agencies, and sharing threat intelligence, investigators can effectively dismantle criminal networks, disrupt illicit operations, and protect communities from emerging digital threats.

Ultimately, the role of digital forensics in law enforcement extends beyond crime investigation to include proactive measures such as digital evidence preservation, cybersecurity awareness, and capacity building within law enforcement agencies. By integrating digital forensic capabilities into broader law enforcement strategies, agencies can enhance public safety, uphold justice, and maintain trust and integrity in the criminal justice system. Examining case examples and the forensic techniques employed reveals the intricate methods and technologies pivotal in uncovering crucial evidence and solving complex investigations across various domains. In a corporate espionage case, investigators utilized `EnCase Forensic` to acquire forensic images (`.e01` files) of suspect laptops, ensuring data integrity and chain of custody by executing commands like `encase acquire -f evidence.e01 -t disk -y`. This allowed them to extract deleted emails, documents, and browser history using `Autopsy` for file system analysis and keyword searches, employing commands such as `autopsy -o /path/to/image.dd` to navigate through forensic images (`image.dd`) and identify pertinent evidence.

Similarly, in a cybercrime investigation involving ransomware, forensic experts deployed `Volatility Framework` to analyze memory dumps (`memdump`), identifying malicious processes and network connections through commands like `volatility -f memdump.raw pslist` to list running processes in a memory dump (`memdump.raw`). This enabled them to reconstruct the attacker's activities and decrypt encrypted files using `Kali Linux` and `John the Ripper`, leveraging commands such as `john --format=zip --wordlist=rockyou.txt encrypted.zip` for brute-force password cracking.

In a child exploitation case, digital forensics specialists employed `Cellebrite UFED` to extract and analyze data from a suspect's smartphone, obtaining call logs, chat conversations, and multimedia files through commands like `cellebrite_ufed --extract all --phone /dev/sdb`. They reconstructed deleted messages using `foremost` for file carving and recovered incriminating photos and videos employing commands like `foremost -t all -i /path/to/image.dd -o /recovery/output`.

Furthermore, in a financial fraud investigation, investigators utilized `X-Ways Forensics` to conduct a thorough examination of suspect computers, identifying altered financial records and uncovering hidden spreadsheets through commands such as `x-ways.exe /extract /all /source C:\SuspectPC\Drive_C`.

In a digital harassment case, digital forensic examiners leveraged `Wireshark` to capture and analyze network traffic (`pcap` files) originating from the suspect's IP address, revealing threatening emails sent through unsecured Wi-Fi networks. They identified the source of malicious emails and tracked the suspect's online activities using `tcpdump -i wlan0 -w capture.pcap` to capture packets on interface `wlan0` and write them to a file `capture.pcap`.

In another scenario involving intellectual property theft, investigators deployed `AccessData FTK` to search for and recover stolen trade secrets from a former employee's laptop, utilizing commands like `ftk imager --capture evidence.ad1 /dev/sdb1` to acquire a forensic image (`evidence.ad1`) of the suspect's hard drive (`/dev/sdb1`). They examined file metadata and accessed timestamp information through commands such as `ftkimager.exe /image e:\SuspectDrive.E01 /output e:\SuspectEvidence -t "keyword"` for extracting specific file types and key terms.

In a terrorism investigation, digital forensics played a crucial role in deciphering encrypted communications and uncovering terrorist networks. Forensic experts employed `TrueCrypt` and `VeraCrypt` to decrypt hidden volumes and recover incriminating documents and communication logs using commands such as `veracrypt -t --pim=0 --protect-hidden=no volume.vc`.

Moreover, in a phishing scam case targeting a financial institution, investigators utilized `MailXaminer` to analyze email headers and attachments, identifying spoofed email addresses and tracing the origin of fraudulent wire transfers through commands such as `mailxaminer -f /path/to/email.pst -e "keyword"` for searching keywords in email archives.

Throughout these diverse cases, the application of digital forensic techniques not only uncovered critical evidence but also played a pivotal role in securing convictions, dismantling criminal networks, and safeguarding organizations against future threats. By leveraging advanced tools and methodologies, digital forensics professionals continue to innovate and adapt to evolving cyber threats, ensuring justice and accountability in the digital age.

## Chapter 10: Case Study: Forensic Analysis of iOS Device in Legal Proceedings

Legal challenges in iOS device forensics present intricate hurdles that digital investigators and legal professionals must navigate with precision and expertise to ensure admissible evidence and uphold due process. One of the primary legal challenges lies in obtaining lawful access to iOS devices, especially when dealing with encrypted data protected by passcodes or biometric authentication. Forensic experts often rely on tools like `GrayKey` or `Cellebrite UFED` to perform physical or logical extractions, using commands such as `graykey acquire` or `cellebrite_ufed --extract all --phone /dev/sdb` to bypass device locks and extract data, adhering to legal guidelines and obtaining proper authorization from courts through warrants or subpoenas.

The legality of accessing cloud-based data linked to iOS devices poses another significant challenge, requiring investigators to navigate privacy laws and obtain appropriate legal permissions. Tools like `Elcomsoft Phone Breaker` or `Celebrite Physical Analyzer` facilitate the extraction of iCloud backups (`Apple ID` and `Password`). Commands such as `elcomsoft_phone_breaker.exe --appleid victim@example.com --password P@ssw0rd --extract --system` enable forensic analysts to access cloud-based data while ensuring compliance with data protection regulations and obtaining user consent or legal authorization as required by law enforcement agencies.

Furthermore, interpreting and presenting digital evidence extracted from iOS devices in court demands a thorough understanding of forensic methodologies and adherence to legal standards for evidence admissibility. Forensic examiners utilize tools like `X-Ways Forensics` or `Autopsy` for file system analysis, keyword searches, and metadata examination. Commands like `x-ways.exe /extract /all /source C:\SuspectPC\Drive_C` or `autopsy -o /path/to/image.dd` help in reconstructing digital timelines and identifying relevant evidence crucial to the case.

Privacy concerns also play a significant role in iOS device forensics, especially regarding the extraction of personal data unrelated to the investigation. Forensic investigators must employ targeted searches and strict data minimization principles, using commands such as `grep -i "keyword" file.txt` or `find /path/to/extracted_data -name "*.pdf"` to locate specific information relevant to the case while respecting the privacy rights of individuals and adhering to legal restrictions on data access and retention.

Chain of custody and data integrity are critical aspects of iOS device forensics, requiring meticulous documentation and procedural adherence to ensure that digital evidence remains untampered and admissible in court. Commands like `dd` or `dc3dd` are used to create forensic images (`dd if=/dev/sda of=image.dd bs=1M`) of storage devices, maintaining data integrity and documenting the acquisition process from initial capture to analysis and presentation in legal proceedings.

Moreover, the evolution of iOS security measures and encryption technologies presents ongoing challenges for forensic investigators, requiring continuous adaptation and innovation in forensic methodologies and tools. Tools such as `Checkm8` exploit iOS vulnerabilities to gain unauthorized access, using commands like `checkm8 -d` to bypass device locks and extract data for forensic analysis, while legal challenges may arise concerning the legality and ethical implications of using such exploits in investigations.

The admissibility of digital evidence extracted from iOS devices hinges on demonstrating forensic rigor and reliability in court, necessitating comprehensive documentation of forensic processes and methodologies. Forensic tools like `Encase Forensic` or `FTK Imager` assist in creating forensic images (`e01` or `aff` files) and conducting detailed examinations of digital artifacts. Commands such as `encase acquire -f evidence.e01 -t disk -y` or `ftkimager.exe /image e:\SuspectDrive.E01 /output e:\SuspectEvidence -t "keyword"` facilitate data acquisition and analysis while adhering to legal standards and guidelines.

Additionally, international legal considerations and jurisdictional issues may complicate iOS device forensics, especially in cases involving cross-border data transfers or multinational investigations. Forensic examiners collaborate with legal experts and law enforcement agencies to navigate international treaties, mutual legal assistance agreements, and data protection regulations, ensuring lawful data access and cooperation across jurisdictions.

Forensic analysis and its courtroom presentation represent a critical juncture where meticulously gathered digital evidence is transformed into compelling legal arguments and factual narratives. The process begins with the acquisition of forensic images (`dd` or `dc3dd`) from devices using commands like `dd if=/dev/sda of=image.dd bs=1M`, ensuring the preservation of data integrity and adherence to chain of custody protocols essential for legal admissibility. These images serve as the foundation for subsequent forensic examinations using tools such as `Autopsy` or `Encase Forensic`, which facilitate file system analysis, keyword searches, and metadata examination to identify relevant evidence crucial to the case.

In preparing digital evidence for courtroom presentation, forensic analysts employ techniques to authenticate and validate the integrity of extracted data, ensuring it withstands scrutiny under cross-examination. Commands such as `hashdeep` or `md5sum` calculate cryptographic hashes (`md5sum /path/to/file`) to verify the integrity of forensic images or extracted files, providing assurance that data has not been tampered with since its acquisition.

Moreover, forensic experts utilize timeline analysis tools like `Sleuth Kit` or `X-Ways Forensics` to reconstruct digital timelines (`fls /path/to/image.dd`) and establish sequences of events relevant to the case, demonstrating the chronology of actions taken on devices and the context in which evidence was generated. These tools enable analysts to correlate timestamps, file access patterns, and user activities, providing a comprehensive narrative that supports legal arguments and aids in presenting a coherent story to the court.

The presentation of digital evidence in court demands clear and persuasive visual aids that effectively convey complex technical information to judges and jurors. Forensic software such as `FTK Imager` or `Volatility Framework` assists in generating forensic reports (`ftkimager.exe /image e:\SuspectDrive.E01 /output e:\SuspectEvidence -t "keyword"`) and visual representations (`volatility -f memdump.raw imageinfo`) of digital artifacts and analysis findings, facilitating comprehension and enhancing the impact of evidence presented during trial.

Furthermore, metadata analysis using tools like `exiftool` or `foremost` helps forensic examiners extract metadata (`exiftool /path/to/file`) embedded within digital files, providing valuable contextual information such as creation dates, GPS coordinates, and device identifiers that strengthen the evidentiary value of digital artifacts. This metadata serves to authenticate the origin and integrity of files presented as evidence, substantiating claims and refuting potential challenges to the authenticity of digital evidence.

In cases involving multimedia evidence, forensic analysts employ `FFmpeg` or `ImageMagick` for media file analysis and enhancement (`ffmpeg -i input.mp4 -vf "scale=640:360" output.mp4`), ensuring clarity and accuracy in presenting videos or images during courtroom proceedings. These tools enable forensic experts to extract frames, enhance quality, and annotate visual evidence to highlight relevant details crucial to the case's narrative.

Cross-examination readiness is a critical aspect of forensic analysis and courtroom presentation, requiring forensic examiners to anticipate and effectively address challenges to their methodologies, findings, and interpretations. Rigorous documentation of forensic processes using contemporaneous notes, forensic reports, and evidence logs (`log2timeline /path/to/image.dd`) provides a verifiable record of investigative steps taken and ensures transparency in the presentation of digital evidence.

Moreover, forensic analysts collaborate closely with legal teams to prepare witnesses for testimony, ensuring they communicate technical details clearly and effectively to non-technical audiences. This preparation includes rehearsing explanations of forensic findings, demonstrating proficiency with forensic tools (`sleuthkit -m /path/to/image.dd`) used in the investigation, and articulating the significance of digital evidence within the broader context of the case.

Legal challenges in the admissibility of digital evidence often hinge on demonstrating the reliability and relevance of forensic methodologies employed. Forensic experts adhere to established forensic standards (`nist_automated`) and guidelines (`iso27043`), ensuring compliance with legal requirements and overcoming objections to the authenticity and integrity of digital evidence presented (`ftk imager -i /path/to/image.dd -o /output -t "keyword"`).

# Conclusion

In this comprehensive book bundle, "iOS Forensics 101: Extracting Logical and Physical Data from iPhone, iPad, and Mac OS," readers have embarked on a journey through the fundamental principles and advanced techniques of digital investigations specific to Apple's ecosystem. Across four essential volumes, each dedicated to different facets of iOS forensics, this collection has provided a thorough foundation and in-depth knowledge essential for navigating the complexities of digital forensics in iOS environments.

"iOS Forensics 101: Introduction to Digital Investigations" lays the groundwork by familiarizing readers with the essential concepts, methodologies, and legal considerations crucial for conducting effective digital investigations on Apple devices. It serves as a primer for understanding the unique challenges and opportunities presented by iOS forensics, setting the stage for deeper exploration.

"iOS Forensics 101: Techniques for Extracting Logical Data" delves into practical techniques and tools used to extract and analyze logical data from iPhones, iPads, and Mac OS devices. From iCloud backups to app data and user-generated content, this volume equips investigators with the skills needed to uncover valuable evidence while maintaining forensic integrity and adhering to legal standards.

"iOS Forensics 101: Mastering Physical Data Acquisition" elevates the reader's expertise by focusing on advanced methods for acquiring physical images of iOS devices. Through detailed exploration of tools such as GrayKey, Cellebrite UFED, and Checkm8, forensic professionals gain proficiency in accessing encrypted data, bypassing device security, and retrieving comprehensive device images crucial for in-depth forensic analysis.

"iOS Forensics 101: Expert Analysis and Case Studies" culminates the bundle with real-world applications, expert insights, and detailed case studies that illustrate the practical application of iOS forensic techniques in solving complex investigations. By examining diverse scenarios—from cybercrimes to corporate espionage and beyond—readers gain a deeper understanding of how forensic methodologies translate into actionable intelligence and courtroom-ready evidence.

Together, these volumes not only equip aspiring and seasoned forensic professionals with technical expertise but also instill a strategic mindset essential for navigating the evolving landscape of digital investigations. As the digital footprint expands and technology evolves, "iOS Forensics 101" remains an indispensable resource, empowering readers to stay at the forefront of iOS forensic methodologies and contribute effectively to the pursuit of justice and truth in the digital age.

www.ingramcontent.com/pod-product-compliance
Lightning Source LLC
Chambersburg PA
CBHW071237050326
40690CB00011B/2151